New Wineskins

A Commentary on Luke's Gospel

Jeff Krogstad

www.jeffkrogstad.com

ISBN: Paperback 978-1-0878-5422-9
       Ebook 978-1-0878-5423-6

For Mathea, remembering with joy so many fascinating, far-ranging discussions.

A few years ago we wandered past the cemetery on Queen Anne Hill up to the bookstore (where else?). As we walked, we imagined reading the gospel of Luke together. This book grew out of that conversation.

Without your delightful curiosity and passionate search for truth, it would remain unwritten.

Love you!

-Dad

Introduction

Think of it as a conversation. Read the passage from Luke's gospel. That's the important part. Then read what I've written here. (Less important, but hopefully helpful.) Then react. Disagree. Argue. Nod. Laugh. Ponder. Discuss. Rinse. Repeat.

Read a few verses a day, or every couple of days. Let Luke's characters come to life in your mind. Especially Jesus. Get to know him. That's a conversation, too.

He makes so clear in this gospel that stuffy old religion can't contain the dynamic new life he wants for his followers. New wine requires new wineskins.

One hope I have is that groups of people who meet in homes (as Luke himself described at the end of Acts 2) might use these thoughts and questions as a way to dig into Luke's gospel together. The Life Groups at The Open Door Christian Church have been much in my mind as I've written and compiled these reflections, especially the "Questions to think about" at the end of each section.

Whatever the conversation, my prayer is that these reflections help us all grow in love with Jesus.

Jeff Krogstad
November 2019

Luke 1:1-4

Odd as it seems, this is one of my very favorite passages of scripture.

It's worth pausing at the beginning of Luke to examine what an old professor of mine used to call "the glasses through which we view the Bible." What do we mean if we use a word like "inspiration" to talk about the Bible? Does that mean it's a magic book, full of secret messages and powerful spiritual forces? Does it mean one must be careful never to put another book (let alone the TV remote) on top of the Bible? Does it mean that just opening the book and letting the pages fall at random and plucking a verse out of context is a legitimate way to hear God speak?

The Bible is without doubt a powerful book and I firmly believe God can use it however he wants. The question we're asking right now, though, is how *best* to view the Bible. How can we most responsibly regard this book?

Luke gives us significant hints here. He starts out by telling us, unlike most biblical authors, about his own writing process. He says a few critically important things in these first verses:

1. Many people in Luke's time had "undertaken to compile a narrative" about the events of Jesus' birth, life, death, and resurrection. There were multiple people trying to get the events recorded.

Luke may have had access to Matthew and Mark, and possibly other written accounts.

2. Luke himself is of the second generation of Jesus-followers—not an eyewitness himself, he has received the narrative from those who were in fact eyewitnesses.

3. Luke is concerned for a third generation of Jesus-followers to be instructed accurately. In Luke's case, he is writing for someone named Theophilus. Given the way Luke addresses Theophilus, he is probably a mid-level Roman official of some kind.

4. Luke has been engaged in his research for some time. He describes himself as "having followed all things closely for some time past" and he is concerned to write "an orderly account." While Luke doesn't describe his research directly, we know from his second volume (Acts) that initially he was a companion of Paul on some of his journeys. From Luke's writing we can see that he apparently dug into sources other gospel writers had not tapped. Perhaps most intriguing, Luke writes a great deal that had to come from Mary (Jesus' mother) herself, and he is not bashful about letting her perspective shine through his narrative.

A word about our own context as we start to read. We are, of course, victims of our own perspectives. So among other things, we have inherited a movement that became popular about 150 years ago and lasted in some ways up to the present day. During this century and a half, scholars felt obligated to discount the biblical accounts as legitimate historical sources. It became popular to scoff at the "historicity" of the biblical accounts, including the gospels, and to say it was impossible that they could be trustworthy narratives. Luke *obviously* fabricated details. That attitude is still to be found in some "scholarly" circles to this day.

Trouble is, Luke has stood the test of academic scrutiny. (So has the rest of the Bible if it is treated responsibly, but that's beyond the scope of this commentary.) Modern archaeology has repeatedly verified Luke's veracity, from the scrupulous listing of political powers in Luke 3:1-2, to Luke's use of the Greek word *politarchoi* (city rulers) in Thessalonica in Acts 17, to detailed descriptions of first century nautical practices and techniques. All these and many more have been independently proved after having been dismissed for decades as fable. These days the cutting edge of scholarly research says that Luke is an incredibly trustworthy historical source. Luke carefully researched and responsibly recorded to the best of his human ability.

And that brings us to the nature of the Bible. Looking at Luke 1:1-4, we have to say that this gospel account is a human book in the deepest, richest sense. It is written by an individual man, a Greek, a physician. He accompanied Paul and hobnobbed with the apostles and with Jesus' own blood relatives. He used careful research techniques and wrote in his well-educated but accessible Greek vocabulary. He had an eye for detail and a concern for the underdog. What's more, Luke has an agenda, and in the face of postmodern critics who are always suspicious of authority because it comes with Agendas, Luke is clear about his. He writes to help a sympathetic Roman official understand Christianity not as a subversive cult, but as a legitimate movement growing out of historical events. These events require a response from Theophilus, and from us.

Given all of Luke's humanity, what does it mean to say that the Gospel according to Luke is "inspired"? Just as the Council of Chalcedon four hundred years later would declare theologically that we must view Jesus as 100% human and 100% divine, Luke's careful artistry compels us to say that the Bible is a human book. But it is also a divine book, a book that (as Luke's friend Paul wrote) is in some sense "God-breathed." That does not make it a magical book, but rather it says something about divine inspiration itself. God tends not to inspire in a magical sense (though miraculous things do indeed happen). Rather, inspiration is a flowing of the Holy Spirit in and through the best efforts of fallible human beings. Luke's careful research and animated narrative bear the undeniable marks of God's fingerprints—in, with and under Luke's own fingerprints all through the text.

Inspiration lies not only in how Luke researched and wrote, but also in how the text has been transmitted to you and me. That inspiration also extends to how you and I read. So when we pick up Luke's narrative, it is entirely appropriate to pray for God to speak, to open our eyes, ears, minds, all our faculties, so that we might gain "certainty concerning the things [we] have been taught." Inspiration creates a divine connection between the reader and the writer and the subjects of the story. Above all, inspiration means that through this text we connect with God himself as his Spirit brings the words to life in us. Thank God for a writer like Luke who not only diligently pursued his own writer's craft, but who also tells us about his agenda, priorities, and process so that we might understand what's going on for him behind the narrative.

Questions to think about:
1. Have you ever had to write a story or a paper? What was that process like for you?
2. Does anything in these first four verses surprise you? What do you think of Luke's approach to writing about Jesus' life, death, and resurrection?
3. How do you react to the idea that the Bible is inspired? Do you gain any understanding of what that means in these verses?
4. Are you comfortable thinking about how human authors used their own effort and skill to shape God's Word? Why / why not?

Luke 1:5-25

Luke does a masterful job in this account of pulling together the threads of the Jewish world and all its hopes. There are echoes of several Old Testament stories here, most notably the birth of Samuel (1 Samuel 1-2) and actions of Elijah (1 Kings 17-2 Kings 2) and the prophecy at the end of Malachi (Malachi 4). Woven in with these stories (and so much more from the Old Testament and

Jewish history) is a sense of the frustrated hopes of the
Jewish people, who were longing for a Messiah. They
longed not necessarily for a religious figure in our sense,
but rather a warrior-prophet who would reinstate the
political state of Israel, much like the Maccabees had done
a century and a half before. It is hard for us even to begin
to understand what it was like for the Jewish people in
these days and how firmly their hopes were wrapped
around the anticipation that God would act decisively to
restore their political state by sending the Messiah. Rabbis
had made a growth industry of interpreting the "seventy
weeks" in the book of Daniel, and all interpreters agreed
that the fulfillment of God's promise was very, very near.

In that anticipation, the temple in Jerusalem bustled.
Estimates are that there were about nine thousand priests
employed by the temple, living throughout the region and
traveling into Jerusalem to serve as their divisions and
their lots were chosen and scheduled. A generation before,
Herod the Great had undertaken to rebuild Ezra's humble
temple, replacing it with a grand vision of massive
stonework. Herod's project was about half finished at the
time of Luke 1, and the people were excited–not about
Herod, who was a violent tyrant disrespected and feared
by all, but about the glory of the temple and the
anticipation that finally, God would return and their
functional exile would end. Exile? Yes, the people had
returned from Babylon five hundred years before, but
God's presence had never returned to Ezra's temple, and
they were waiting for God's presence, God's action, God's
messenger, God's Messiah. What's more, no prophet had
appeared for almost four hundred years speaking God's

words with authority. Since Malachi and a few other minor prophets, the heavens had been silent.

In that context, Luke tells us an amazing amount of detail about Zechariah and Elizabeth. They are firmly established as far as the Jewish concerns about genealogy. Their pedigrees are perfect. They are righteous, not tainted by the graft and cynicism that had grown up around the all-consuming temple industry in Jerusalem. Even as the Jews waited in hope, we gain an excruciating glimpse into the frustrated longings of Zechariah and Elizabeth and their heartbroken yearning for a child. (This story echoes that of Elkanah and Hannah and the birth of Samuel in 1 Samuel very strongly, and that theme continues through Luke 1.) Zechariah is chosen by lot to burn incense. He is not, as many preachers have said, going into the Holy of Holies on the Day of Atonement (Yom Kippur). He is simply going into the Holy Place, immediately outside the Holy of Holies, where the altar of incense was placed. Burning incense on the altar of incense was a daily occurrence, and it was surrounded by an important time of prayer when people would gather outside and offer their prayers while the priest fulfilled the duty of burning a handful of incense on the coals. So for a few minutes, Zechariah is all alone in the very heart of Jerusalem, in the heart of the temple, alone with his prayers, alone with his hopes, alone with his frustrated longing and a handful of smelly incense.

And in that moment, God shows up. God shows up via his messenger, an angel. The angel speaks powerful promises that address all Zechariah's hopes and fears, that affirm and verify the longings of his people and that comfort

12

Zechariah, this righteous man, in his own longing. Or at least they should. But Zechariah has lived so long in frustrated hope that his response to the angel is, quite literally, "Says who?" Most translations, tragically, tone down the scathing bitterness of Zechariah's response to something like the ESV's "How shall I know this?" The Greek is *kata ti* which means "according to who?"

It is hard to wait in hope. It is hard to hear God promise good things and not see tangible evidence that those promises are moving toward fruition. In the wisdom of God, human life contains so many seasons that fall between planting and reaping, between the longing and the fulfillment, between the promise and the reality. It seems God's standard operating procedure to give a vision, but then (as Oswald Chambers says) to take us from the mountaintop of vision down into the valley of drudgery where God beats us into shape to receive the vision he has given. The struggle for us is to remain open to the fulfillment, not to close our hearts either by growing cynical or by settling for the also-ran of our own paltry efforts. What are we willing to settle for? Do we dare wait fully extended in hope, and risk appearing a fool if God doesn't show up? And when an opportunity arises to step toward the fulfillment of our longings, can we step toward them decisively, firmly, faithfully?

In a severe mercy, Gabriel (we gain a tantalizing glimpse into the courts of heaven through Gabriel's description of himself and his station) strikes Zechariah dumb. Gabriel's response and its tone make sense if we understand what Zechariah has asked and the disrespectful tone of his question. Gabriel *stands* in the presence of God, where every human falls to the ground. Gabriel comes not in his own authority, but by the direct command and plan of God. God is moving, fulfilling the word he has spoken generations before. Who are you, Zechariah, to doubt God's promises? Since you see fit to speak so disrespectfully, your mouth is closed until you see the child and act to name him in faith, in obedience to this vision.

It is comforting that Zechariah is not discarded for his disrespect. God still uses him to become the father of John the Baptist, the forerunner of the Messiah. In the fulfillment of the vision, Zechariah himself gains a difficult gift. Instead of being free to tell people that now God is working to fulfill his long promises, Zechariah is silent. He receives the time of Elizabeth's pregnancy as a time of reflection, of pondering, of waiting. Silence. While he watches her belly swell and the fulfillment of the promise grow, he has time to reflect on his own attitudes and to repent, as his son will call the nation to repentance.

But before the birth of John, we get an alternative example of how to respond when God comes to announce the fulfillment of his plans. More on that in the next section.

Questions to think about:
1. Would you say you are by nature a patient person? Why / why not?
2. What does it feel like to wait for God during times of frustration?

3. Read Gabriel's description of what Zechariah's son will accomplish. How might you feel if you were Zechariah, hearing this? (See Luke 1:15-17)
4. Does God's judgment on Zechariah seem fair to you? Why / why not?

Luke 1:26-45

Mary's response to the angel's announcement provides a powerful contrast with Zechariah's pained cynicism. And here we first experience one of Luke's distinctive qualities among the gospels: The movement Jesus began was always powerful for women. He opened doors of opportunity and status that had long been closed in Judaism and paganism and Greco-Roman culture. Writing this gospel, Luke especially champions women as role models. They are portrayed as faithful followers of Jesus. So Mary, who has very little power in Jewish circles of her day, becomes an incredible model of trust for us.

Not that Mary is perfect. The whole business of "venerating" Mary (making her a fourth member of the Trinity, etc.) that has been done through the years is wholly without biblical warrant. Mary is powerful for us precisely because of her accessible humanity, not because of some exalted quasi-divine status as "redemptrix" or any of that. Mary is a young Jewish girl, learning and growing, full of the insecurities and limitations and hopes that are common to humans in that period between childhood and adulthood. She's probably in her mid-teens when Gabriel finds her, though we don't know for certain.

Make no mistake about this story: the announcement Gabriel brings will cause trouble and discomfort and social upheaval and relational distress to Mary. When God starts to move in our lives, these things follow. Why? We tend to create stable systems that obey human laws and restrictions, that help us avoid shame, that keep our self-respect intact. And God tends to break those systems.

In some English translations Mary's question sounds a lot like Zechariah's, but the two could not be more different in Greek. In contrast to Z's "Says who?" Mary asks a question borne out of genuine desire to understand and to be obedient. There is not a hint of bitterness or rebelliousness or cynicism when she asks her question, just honest confusion that longs to trust. Her question is a good example of what Anselm centuries later would call "faith seeking understanding." Mary, betrothed to Joseph, understands where babies come from. Does this mean they should speed up the wedding? Will there be some other human agency to initiate this pregnancy? No, Gabriel says, this is going to be a unique pregnancy, a Holy Spirit initiated embryo that will grow in her. Such things were common in Greek mythology, though the squabbling, venal Greek gods themselves were a far cry from the Jews' One Holy God. The focus here is not on any kind of sexual encounter between God and Mary—far from it—but rather on the incarnation itself, on God becoming human. That is where the focus will remain throughout the story, and the encounter between Mary and Gabriel sets the stage.

Mary's willing, trusting obedience sets a challenge before us. What is my response when God shows up and invites me into something greater, more risky, more disruptive than I have planned? Am I willing, or horrified? Do I welcome God's plans, though they may complicate my life, or do I retreat into the comfort of my own agenda? Mary doesn't know up front all that this announcement will cost her, but she is willing and ready to jump into what God has for her. And through Mary, God is at work for the rest of his creation, for all of us. In a lesser way, this is the invitation of God to each of us today. He comes to us with an announcement that he is ready to become enfleshed in our flesh, to take up residence in our lives, to make himself a reality to the world in and through us. How will we respond? Will we be willing, even eager, to let God's love become an incarnate reality in us, that his love might be visible to the world through us? Mary leads us here.

And yet even for Mary, prudence dictates that she makes the journey to stay with her cousin Elizabeth for a few months. She gets out of town before that baby bump shows up, before the betrothal with Joseph needs to be called off (we see that from Joseph's perspective in Matthew's gospel). Mary is not superhuman. She needs the encouragement of her older cousin Elizabeth, whose swelling belly becomes the tangible reminder of God's goodness and faithfulness to fulfill his abundant promises. Elizabeth in her joy and her humility becomes a witness, a mentor, an encouragement for Mary; their babies together will shake the foundations of the Jewish nation and the world.

Questions to think about:
1. How might Mary have felt when she heard Gabriel's announcement?
2. What would Mary experience as a pregnant single girl in a small town?
3. How does God break down our self-protective structures?
4. Has God ever asked you to do something risky or potentially embarrassing? What happened?

Luke 1:46-56

Mary's song is traditionally called "The Magnificat" because of the first Latin word that translates, "My soul magnifies ..." It's a beautiful song, strongly parallel to Hannah's prayer in 1 Samuel 2. In both cases, the song / prayer is a powerful statement of what it means that God "saves."

Sadly, the whole idea of saving / being saved / salvation has become overlaid with all kinds of religious baggage in our time. In most Christian circles, "being saved" has something to do with being certain you will go to heaven after you die. It is purely individualistic, purely "spiritual" in the sense that it has little or nothing to do with physical reality here and now. Let us be clear: this self-focused version of "being saved" has little to do with a biblical view of salvation.

The word itself comes from the same root as "salve" in our language, and in both Greek and English has to do with healing. Part of the reason this word, this concept, is so hard for us these days is we have little agreement about "sin," little agreement about what it is that we need to be saved from. People who simply focus on morality seem to see salvation as being saved from moral failings so that one can become a good person. The Bible has plenty to say about morality and moral failures, but most of the Bible's content in this regard is telling embarrassing stories about how the greatest heroes have failed. If you come open-eyed to the Bible with the assumption that being saved equals becoming good, you'll get frustrated in a hurry.

Two thoughts that are perhaps helpful.

First, being saved has to do, as we just observed, with healing. Think of all the ways our lives are broken: Broken dreams, broken relationships, broken hopes, broken bodies. Brokenness is a daily reality for every one of us. To be "saved"–that is, to be healed–means that our brokenness is dealt with in an effective way. Wholeness is the opposite of brokenness, and wholeness is a good translation of the Hebrew word "shalom" which most often gets translated as peace. Think of peace not as the absence of conflict, but the presence of wholeness, of the restoration of health in every sense, especially relationally. At our deepest core, our relationship with God is broken as well. Jesus comes to heal that deepest brokenness, and out of that healing, the rest of our lives begin to get set right.

Relationships are the deepest dimension of our lives. This is obvious to anyone who thinks for even a few minutes about it. Consider all the brokenness in our relational lives–between bosses and employees, between husbands and wives, between parents and children, between priests and parishioners, between humans and creation, between managers and the money they manage, between longings and fulfillment... all of these pairings are relational, and all of them are broken. To be saved means to have our relationships put back on the right footing, including our relationship with God. Because of the brokenness in every other area of our lives, we are prone to project onto God all the disappointment, all the shame, all the scolding and frowning and abuse and hateful behavior we experience in every other area that leaves us so deeply broken. God becomes the abusive father, the angry lover, the disappointed mother. But these are our pictures, not reality.

The second thought that might be helpful–and this is really key when one begins to understand the Bible's perspective–is that God is the hero of the story. So much of our striving is built around making ourselves the hero. We strive to look good, to be well thought of, to Do Things Right, to profit, to climb, to endure–all so that we might look like the hero in our own stories. Salvation starts with acknowledging that God is the hero of the story, and it is this more than anything that Mary gets right in the Magnificat. She understands that it is God who has acted to bring healing, that it is God who has power, that it is God who deserves credit. God is the hero. If we want to understand the significance of these stories about Jesus, it starts with recognizing that God is acting for the benefit of his people, his creation, his beloved. God is bringing healing and wholeness where before there was only hopeless brokenness.

To bring this kind of healing, God acts in surprising ways. He gets into the mess, gets dirty to make things happen. Not long ago our church hosted Vacation Bible School. One evening more than a hundred kids showed up and received sparkling white t-shirts and had a great time singing on the beach and playing games and learning about Jesus. Then, in a surprising incarnational move, they were given buckets of colored paint and sponges and played relay races that left those t-shirts a cacophony of color. THEN six adults–yours truly included–donned hooded white painting coveralls and goggles, and buckets of powder paint came out. Each child received a dixie cup, and the powder paint began to fly like a blizzard of many colors. More than anything else, these children seemed absolutely delighted that the adults were getting into the mess with them, getting into the multicolored arena and playing without saying, "Stay inside the lines" and "Make sure you don't get that in your hair" and "NOT IN YOUR MOUTH!" Rather, instead of boundaries designed to shame, the joy of the whole experience was that it was a lot chaotic and everyone ended up full of paint. It's a tiny parable of God getting into the mess with us, less obsessive about keeping us neat and tidy and more about loving the relationship, delighting in the crazy process, joyful to see us growing, healing, learning to fly. After all, he's the one who provided all that paint in the first place.

Questions to think about:
1. As you read Mary's song, what strikes you most?
2. How is it ironic that a single teenage pregnant girl should sing this song?
3. Have you ever seen God break down power structures? What is that like?
4. How well do you deal with messy situations?

Luke 1:57-80

We so often take for granted these intimate scenes that are common throughout the Bible, but so very rare in the rest of ancient literature. We gain a glimpse not only into John's birth, but also into the pained conversations that must have happened between Elizabeth and Zechariah. Likely Zechariah had to use a writing tablet of some kind to converse with his wife. The rest of the community had probably been out of conversation with silent Zechariah since he became mute.

The circumcision of a firstborn male was a major event within the circle of friends and neighbors that surrounded this couple. No doubt there had been many quiet conversations behind closed doors about oh, how tragic it is that Elizabeth is barren, they're such a nice couple, why would God do such a thing? And now here they are, circumcising their firstborn and the entire community came to celebrate with them.

But even here in the midst of their joy, God's plan struck a sour note: "His name is John." The community expected that the naming of the boy would honor the family, would honor Zechariah's lineage. But "John" is not a family name. Yet God has demanded this, and Zechariah and Elizabeth are agreed. His name is John. Like Samuel a thousand years before, this child will never really belong to his parents. Luke tells us as much when he concludes this chapter: John was "in the wilderness." Whether this refers to the Essenes at Qumran (who are never directly mentioned in the Bible) or to some other dimension of preparing this prophet, we don't know. John's teaching and practice will have a lot in common with the Essenes, but that detail lies beyond our knowledge.

We do know that John is set apart for God's work. He is Elijah reborn, not in the sense of literal reincarnation but in the sense of the prophetic archetype. He will prepare the way for the Messiah. He will lead the revival among the Jewish people that turns their hearts back to the Lord in preparation for God to visit and redeem them (1:68).

Zechariah's song points out how different our understanding has become. We carefully separate church from state, religion from politics, finances from recreation, family from the wider community, and all the rest. Our lives are full of lines that keep things in their proper categories. For the first century Jews, however (and for most of the rest of humanity through history), things blend together like the different ingredients of a stew. We share each others' flavors and influence each other. So the anticipation of the Messiah was religious and political and relational and military and devotional, without dividing one from the other. The gathering around John's circumcision is a spiritual event but it is also a party and it is also deeply traditionally religious and it is political. So Zechariah's song crosses all these boundaries and back again. It is completely, entirely about God getting into the mess of every sphere of life, without exception. When Zechariah speaks (v. 77) about the forgiveness of sins, everyone in earshot knew that it was their sins that took them into Babylonian exile five hundred years before. It was their sins, still standing between them and God, that allowed the Romans to dominate their land at the present time. Those sins were not merely political; they were deeply spiritual.

The realities of everyday life do not fall into neat categories. If our relationship with God is out of whack, every dimension of our lives will be strained and skewed. Repentance, then, involves a turning back to God who stands at the center of every dimension of life. We surrender everything to him: our political views, spiritual practices, dietary habits, alcohol consumption, extended family relationships, local community structures, marriages, parenting, attitudes about other countries and other races, beliefs about the deepest questions of life and death. We surrender all of this and more to God, recognizing his kingship over us. God will not tolerate being cordoned off into one "spiritual" area of life. This is the message in Zechariah's song, and this is the message John will proclaim once he appears publicly in Israel. It is the message we still need to hear two thousand years later.

Questions to think about:

1. Why is it so uncomfortable to talk in polite company about things like politics and religion?
2. How does Zechariah's song mix those potent categories?
3. If you could, what is one thing you'd ask God to change in our world today?
4. What makes it challenging to surrender our lives to God as King?

Edging into Luke 2

Some parts of the Bible are so familiar it is hard to read them well. That is certainly the case with Luke 2:1-20. For many of us it is nearly impossible to read these verses without imagining a Sunday School Christmas program, bathrobes and cardboard crowns and the innkeeper solemnly shaking his head. Or maybe you hear Linus reciting these verses in the Peanuts Christmas special. Or perhaps like me, the words, "In those days a decree went out from Caesar Augustus..." launch you into a memory of family Christmas Eves, Dad reading the familiar story while us kids shook with excitement to open presents.

These memories and associations are not bad things, but they keep us from really hearing the verses. And the Sunday School imagery includes all kinds of visuals that frankly are nowhere to be found in the text.

Luke's original readers in the first century would have resonated with the idea that Caesar Augustus (and subsequent Caesars) could simply pronounce an edict that moved populations. Joseph and Mary are caught up in the requirements of Caesar's rule, and everyone who read this gospel was familiar with the Roman census. It was customary for Rome to require a census every 14 years. There is a well-documented census in 6-7 AD, and if the 14 year pattern held, a census declared in 8-7 BC would do nicely for our purposes–meaning that allowing some time for the wheels of administrative purpose to grind into motion, Jesus was probably born around 6-5 BC. Thousands of paragraphs, pages, books have been written about the possible dating of Jesus' birth, and we won't dig too far into it here.

For our purposes at the moment, though, consider the complete ordinariness of this story, and how God is involved in the mundane. Have you ever considered that God can use the IRS or your tax return? Have you imagined that a presidential executive order, a home refinance program, or a student loan policy might be used by God to shape your life? Even Caesar, according to Luke, is used by God to accomplish his purposes. In this case, the census fulfills a 600-year-old prophecy that the Messiah will be born in Bethlehem.

God is moving, and he sometimes acts through the most mundane of factors. The trick for us is to be seeking him. God will do whatever is needful to set us free to seek him. As Oswald Chambers says, people "pour themselves into creeds, and God has to blast them out of their prejudices before they can become devoted to Jesus Christ."

Luke 2:1-7

As I sit down to write this, the skies are gray and it looks like late evening, even though it's noon. Heavy clouds hang overhead, and for the last twelve hours, thunderheads have been pounding this part of the world. It's tempting to describe the weather in apocalyptic terms, especially when I heard this morning that a small town not far away got eight inches of rain last night. Though we didn't get nearly that amount, I didn't sleep much, listening to the rain pound the roof over my head and watching lightning flash the oak trees outside my window into stark relief against the lake. I had long hours to lay awake thinking and watching. It was a spectacular night.

There are lots of ways to describe the same scene. I could wax eloquent about darkness at midday, or I could analyze the cumulonimbus clouds and the prevailing winds, or I could make a joke about building an ark.

The gospel writers describe God becoming human in diverse ways. John goes back to the language of Genesis, starting with "In the beginning ..." Matthew emphasizes the entirety of the Old Testament story and tells the awkward tale of this illegitimate pregnancy from Joseph's perspective. For a completely different version of the Christmas story writ large as a Tolkien epic complete with a dragon, check out Revelation 12.

Luke, on the other hand, stays mostly with Mary's perspective and tells things from as factual a stance as possible, emphasizing how Mary and Joseph travel to Bethlehem in obedience to Caesar's edict. (Luke is, recall, writing to a Roman official arguing, at least in part, that this Jesus-movement is not a threat to Rome, at least in the political or military sense.) In that same factual tone, Luke tells us that "while they were there, the time came for her to give birth." As much as we enjoy the dramatic scene of Joseph and Mary screeching into town with Mary already in labor on the back of a donkey, that's not in the text. We like dramatic timing, but all we know from Luke's account is that at some point while they were in Bethlehem, Mary's baby was born. Similarly, we have no innkeeper to blame for their lodging in a stable. Luke doesn't mention any stable, for that matter. And though the ESV and other translations keep the term "inn," the Greek word that means a place where just anyone can rent a room (like in the parable of the Good Samaritan in Luke 10) is not used here. Rather, the word is better translated "guest room."

In all likelihood, looking at the culture of the time and the information we have in the Bible, Joseph still had extended family living in Bethlehem and it would have been unthinkable not to stay with them. Most Jewish houses of this era had a common living area with one or possibly two separate bedrooms. In a lower portion of the house, separated from the common living room by a step down and probably by a long, low manger, a few animals were kept. So while it wreaks havoc with Sunday School Christmas programs, what likely happened was that Joseph and a very pregnant Mary arrived in Bethlehem and stayed with some of his cousins. Because other guests with higher social standing were already in the home, Joseph and Mary slept in the common room. When Jesus was born there was no place to lay him except in the feed trough.

Maybe not. Maybe the cave you can visit in Bethlehem to this day is the actual place of Jesus' birth. In the end, it doesn't matter much. Still, we need to try, hard as it is, to read the Bible for what it actually says. It is difficult not to bring our assumptions (romanticized or cynical or whatever) to the text.

In any case, Jesus was born in a small village a few miles from the bustling metropolis of Jerusalem, to a not-quite-married couple who were displaced by Augustus' demand that all the world should be registered for taxation and military purposes. His mother, who didn't legally need to travel to Bethlehem, was probably relieved to be out from under the watchful eye of the gossips in Nazareth. Still, she was likely lonely, afraid, and feeling caught up in matters far beyond her control. She could feel, if not see, that dragon (see Revelation 12, referenced above) waiting to devour her and the baby she bore. But even in these chaotic events and feelings, God is in control. He's been working for hundreds of years to heal his broken creation, to reconcile his alienated people. This birth is the first move in the climactic phase of the story he is writing. Next we'll gain just a glimpse of how God himself wants to announce these events, and to whom.

Questions to think about:
1. What is your first Christmas memory? How old were you?
2. How do you react to the idea that some of our traditional Christmas pageants don't accurately reflect the Bible's text?
3. What seems most important in these verses?
4. What is it like to imagine God moving in the great economic and political shifts of our day?

Luke 2:8-21

Many years ago I attended a Christmas concert that included, among other excellent things, a haunting arrangement in Latin of a song that began with a triumphant "Gloria in excelsis Deo" (Glory to God in the highest). Then, at a precise moment, the music turned somber and a thin voice sang "et in terra pax hominibus" (and on earth peace among humans). The announcement of the angel stands counterpoint to our daily reality: There is little peace on earth, and one wonders who those humans are on whom God's favor rests.

The angel has appeared to Zechariah and to Mary, and each has heard the admonition not to be afraid. Now, for the first time in Luke (and a rarity in all of scripture) the angel appears before multiple people, and then is joined by "a multitude of the heavenly host." It seems that the announcements are changing in character as well as in breadth. This time instead of announcing what will happen, the angels come to proclaim what *has* happened. "Unto you is born this day in the city of David a Savior, which is Christ the Lord."

The shepherds are an unlikely audience for such an announcement. They are low on the social hierarchy, tied to their ignominious work, ritually unclean. But as we should expect by now, God chooses that which is unlikely, even disgraced. They respond in trust and obedience. "Let us go to Bethlehem and see this thing that has happened, which the Lord has made known to us." It is likely lambing season, else the sheep would be in the fold overnight, not in the hills. Do all the shepherds come, or do they leave some to tend the birthing ewes? The Old Testament is full of shepherd imagery, from David himself to many passages within the prophets (e.g., see Ezekiel 34). For a number of reasons, God has a special tenderness for sheep and shepherds.

These days, if you visit Bethlehem, its dominating feature is a massive wall that nearly encircles the city. It's a wall of self-protection. It divides the Palestinian West Bank (including Bethlehem proper) from Israel, out of concern that bombers and knife-wielding fanatics will attack the Jewish state and its people. These fears are not without cause. But there can be little better example of how desperately we need a Savior. We need to be reconciled to God and to one another. The walls of enmity and hostility need to be broken down. The spiritual powers of hate and alienation need to be defeated in and for us. All of that language is found in Paul's explanations of what happened at the cross when this swaddled infant was crucified thirty-some years later.

So the announcement of the angels is not a wistful longing that there should be peace. Instead it is a confident proclamation that the plan of God to deal with human sin, to heal the brokenness of his creation, has been put into play. This is not a tender nativity scene as much as it is the opening invasion in a war; less a Christmas concert than it is the bloody landings at Omaha beach.

Et in terra pax hominibus. Truth is, the angels tell us, this is all of us. We are the ones God loves, the ones with whom God is pleased. He invites us to join the chorus and proclaim his radical, healing love to all the broken of creation. Our proclamation is based not on a beautiful Christmas story but on the radical self-giving love of God. He will not stop until he has taken our brokenness into himself so that we might be healed.

Questions to think about:
1. What is the messiest job you've ever had?
2. What reasons can you imagine why God might choose the shepherds for his announcement?
3. How do the shepherds respond to seeing the infant Jesus?
4. What is Mary's reaction to the shepherds? How can we learn from both Mary and the shepherds?

Luke 2:22-40

The news of Jesus' birth continues to spread. Like the shepherds, Anna and Simeon have bandwidth to listen.

While we may often wish God would speak, we rarely assess our own capacity to hear. Yet this idea of capacity is critically important throughout the Bible. "I just want God to speak to me like he did to Moses–to show up in a burning bush. If he did, I would certainly obey." We say things like this, mostly joking, but we perceive a significant disconnect between ourselves and biblical characters who heard God speaking. So with Simeon and Anna in this passage. How did they hear? How did they know?

Yet when Jesus is an adult preaching to his people, he frequently puts the burden back on his hearers. "The one who has ears, let them hear," he often says. It is a provocative challenge: Do we have ears?

Read the biblical texts more closely. Why did those people hear, and others did not? So often, the ones who heard had room for Jesus' words. There was margin in their lives. Shepherds sat on the quiet hillside staring at the stars night after night. Simeon and Anna stayed in the temple constantly seeking God. Moses spent forty years herding sheep in the wilderness, and when the burning bush showed up he watched for a significant amount of time before he noticed anything strange was going on. Read Exodus 3 and you'll see it's because the bush was not consumed by the fire that Moses decided to investigate. How long did it take him to realize the bush wasn't burning up? Ten minutes? Twenty? In that time most of us would have traveled miles down the highway and run three or four more errands. That strange burning bush would be in the rearview mirror and might at best be fodder for dinner conversation later in the day. But Moses, like the shepherds and Simeon and Anna in Luke 2, had bandwidth. He cultivated habits of listening. He had ears.

What is perhaps most surprising in the account is how normal everything is for Joseph and Mary. They are managing the mundane details of naming, of circumcising, of purification, of travel, of childrearing. It almost sounds in the story like they are more often than not preoccupied with the daily details of life. These periodic announcements from God astonish them, calling them back to remember that God is up to something.

We tend to slide back into a deceptive sense that life is simply normal. No matter what God has promised, we need to pick up groceries, go to work, clean the bathroom, watch the news. And we get complacent with the idea that God has made us great and powerful promises precisely because we don't see immediate fulfillment. We're not capable of living on the heights, staring God's plans in the face. Maybe that's a good thing. God gives us the gift of normalcy. The trick for us is not to forget in the face of the mundane details that God is still up to something. He is fulfilling his promises. He is at work in and through and around us, and his promises are good. "Having ears" starts with cultivating times of silence and listening on a daily basis. Then, amidst the clutter, we need to intentionally remind ourselves of what we have heard and seen in those times of listening. If we can learn this habit over time, it creates in us a spirit of watchfulness, a posture of listening. Like Anna and Simeon, then, we can perceive when God shows up, and the conversation with him about his work becomes a daily source of hope and expectation.

Questions to think about:
1. What is the longest you have gone without speaking? What was it like to be silent?
2. Reread Simeon's words. How do you think Joseph and Mary felt when they heard them?
3. If God spoke to you, what do you think he would say?
4. What would it take for you to create times of silence, of margin, in your life?

Luke 2:41-52

It's hard to translate literally what Jesus says in verse 49 about himself. Very likely here (as he will later) he chooses his words carefully. Most English translations prefer "in my Father's house." Some go with "about my Father's business." The Greek is a difficult expression—*en tois tou patros mou*. "In those of my father' is a fair literal rendering but unsatisfying in English. The Greek here lacks any word for "house" or "business." The weak noun "*tois*" implies some kind of content—the things of my father, perhaps. Either sense, the temple (house) or the affairs (business), will suffice on a surface reading.

What is perhaps notable is that Jesus, at twelve years old, recognizes that God is up to stuff. God has an agenda and a set of priorities in this moment. There are ways of spending time that do not align with the things of God, and there are ways of spending time that do. In his adult preaching, this idea will grow and flourish into the center of Jesus' teaching: "the kingdom of God," which again is a poor English rendering of something that Jesus makes immeasurably deep and significant. Many things are incorporated in Jesus' teaching about the kingdom of God. It includes God's sovereignty, the obedient community living in harmony with God's will, restoration of wholeness, and much more. At twelve, teetering on the edge of adulthood in Jewish society of the time, Jesus senses himself called to be in the things of his Father.

Of course there are questions we'd like to ask. Had Mary and Joseph told Jesus the story of his remarkable conception? What were the questions and answers he bantered about with the Jewish teachers? Was this a singular incident, or typical of his childhood? This incident in Luke's narrative is the only detail we have from Jesus' youth. A couple centuries later, the Gnostics would make a growth industry out of fabricating spectacular stories of Jesus as a child. They imagined clay sparrows brought miraculously to life, a playmate struck dead and then resurrected. These stories have no discernible basis in fact, and they don't ring true to the sense of the canonical gospels. There's no call to take them seriously, especially when doing so compromises and contradicts what we know of Jesus from the earliest sources. But we yearn to know more.

One more word of all those in this story. While Jesus speaks in less than clear terms about what he means by his Father's business / house, he is absolutely clear in another word he uses. *Dei* in Greek is a word for necessity. English translates the phrase "I must be" or "I need to be" and in Greek this is a strong imperative statement. Jesus considers this necessary, not optional. He has not willfully chosen an option, disregarding his parents' concerns. He is not acting on a whim. It is absolutely needful that he should be pursuing the things of his Father. A few years later he will state this more fully for his followers. "Seek first the kingdom of God and his righteousness" (Matthew 6:33). At twelve, Jesus is following this command himself.

It is less than helpful to imagine Jesus in a superhero role here, omniscient at twelve years old, knowing all secrets and the like. We distance ourselves from him when we view him in this way. Luke and the other gospel writers are at pains to show Jesus in his full humanity, and that means that at twelve, he is a maturing child, beginning to grasp his identity as a man. He is sensing how God has wired him and what his life will be about. This story at its best pushes us to consider our own necessity, to consider what those things of God are that have been hardwired into our own awareness. What is needful for you to be doing today? What is the business of your heavenly Father that you need to be concerned about? None of us is capable of wrapping our hearts around the entire counsel of God, but he has given each of us a corner of his kingdom with which to concern ourselves. He has given each of us a voice. Can you find yours? Without doubt, there will be others who share that area of interest. Part of the joy of being about your Father's business is the joy of harmonizing your voice with others who see things from a similar vantage point. This might be one reason why Jesus stayed in the temple after his extended family left for Nazareth. He was immersed in joyful conversation about the things of God with others who shared his passion. None of us, not even Jesus, was intended to pursue this kingdom alone.

Yet Luke also tells us that Jesus knew the vision wasn't fulfilled. He submitted to his parents and returned to Nazareth, and so the tantalizing glimpse draws to a close. We long to know the mundane details of Jesus at fifteen, at twenty, at twenty-five. It frustrates us that the next view we'll get is of the adult Jesus sensing that the time has come to begin his ministry. The impetus for that will be his cousin John's voice ringing through the Jordan valley with a call to repentance.

Questions to think about:
1. What was your life like when you were twelve? What was important to you?
2. Have you ever lost track of a child? What was that like for you as a parent or caregiver?
3. If someone asked you what God really cares about, how might you answer?
4. What might it mean for you today to "seek God's kingdom" or to be "about your Father's business"?

Luke 3:1-2

In these two verses, Luke lays out a careful sense of the power structures in place when John begins to preach, starting with Emperor Tiberius. He is careful not to disparage any of these powers–it just wouldn't do to offend Rome. Luke's original readers would have known that about this time, Tiberius (who never really wanted to be Caesar, it seems) had actually removed himself from Rome. For the last decade of his reign, Tiberius left the reins of the Empire to an administrator. He was known as "the gloomiest of men." Pilate by contrast was ruthless, resenting his assignment to the troublesome backwater province of Judea. Pilate did not hesitate to shed Jewish blood in order to keep the peace. The Herodian dynasty had faded from its former brutal glory under Herod the Great (the Herod of the murder of the innocents in Bethlehem around the time of Jesus' birth, see Matthew 2). Now his sons Herod Antipas and Herod Philip served not as kings but as frustrated "tetrarchs" at the pleasure of Rome. They had to balance their self-indulgent habits with the frustrations of ruling without the freedom to make real decisions. In each and every case, these names carry a sense of the fallibility of human rulers and our desperate need for something more–for God to come and set the world to rights, as N.T. Wright likes to put it.

Luke gets a bit more pointed in that regard by mentioning "the high priesthood of Annas and Caiaphas." He feels a little more free to hint at the scandal surrounding this family, who had purchased the high priesthood from Rome. According to Jewish law they were not even eligible to hold the office. What's more, Annas, Caiaphas' father, shared the office with his son and the two passed it back and forth for political advantage as needed. They were skilled politicians who knew how to curry Roman favor. It was these two who presided over Jesus' trial, and it was

Caiaphas in John's gospel who said it was prudent that one man (Jesus) should die for the nation. Caiaphas believed it was better to risk killing the Messiah rather than having Rome come and destroy their country and their temple. Of course, that is exactly what happened in 70 AD.

Lysanias is worth mentioning in some detail. Josephus is by far our most detailed extra-biblical historian for the Jews of this period. He tells of a Lysanias who was tetrarch of Abilene (a region in what we would call the Golan Heights, on the border between northern Israel and southern Lebanon) around 40 BC. (This is fully two generations before the events Luke is describing.) A century or two ago it was popular for scholars to point this out and poke fun at Luke's accuracy. He had obviously thrown Lysanias into the list just to bolster it, without any concern for historical veracity. More recently, however, inscriptions have come to light from the reign of Tiberius mentioning another Lysanias. This was probably the son or grandson of the one Josephus mentions, and he was tetrarch of Abilene at precisely the time Luke is talking about. Always be careful about saying the Bible can't be trusted because some human authority says it's wrong!

One of the benefits of Luke's careful list is that for readers ancient and modern, it places the preaching of John and the ministry of Jesus in a very specific historical context. The list itself served in ancient times to pinpoint when these events took place. Luke's gospel is not about timeless spiritual truths, but about a specific set of historical events tied to a real person. God does not become incarnate in principles, but in history. According to our dating systems, we would say that these events launch onto the historical stage in the late 20's AD.

The point, however, of this tremendous list of human authorities, disappointing and corrupt, comes right at the end of verse two. With all these characters scrambling around the halls of power political and religious, the word of God comes not to Caesar, not to Annas, but to John the son of Zechariah in the wilderness. God is working, and he is no respecter of human power structures. The greatest movement in history starts with John the Baptist, a man who by all appearances has no power, who appears not in the palaces or the temples but in the wilderness. John is preaching not "peace and security"–the slogan of the Caesars (see 1 Thessalonians 5:3)–but repentance for the forgiveness of sins. That phrase will provide the bookends of Luke's story of Jesus' ministry, and that's the topic we'll take up next.

Questions to think about:
1. Who is your favorite American president? Who is your least favorite? Why?
2. Why do you think it is important that Jesus arrives at a particular time in history? See Galatians 4:4.
3. Have you ever seen God choose less-than-powerful people to do his work?
4. John receives the word of God "in the wilderness." Why might this be important?

Luke 3:3-6

A little knowledge is a dangerous thing. But it can be thought provoking, too. I am no scholar of Greek; I know just enough to get myself in trouble, and to get me thinking, which are often the same thing.

Many years ago I noticed the strange construction of the phrase in Luke 3:3. John was proclaiming a baptism of repentance that had something to do with the forgiveness of sins. It was the relationship between repentance and forgiveness that caught me short. The Greek preposition connecting them is *eis* which is generally translated "into." Here, though, it is usually translated "for." Does it make any difference?

Being baptized "for" the forgiveness of your sins implies causality, at least in English. Because you are baptized, you are assured that your sins are forgiven, or maybe even because you are baptized, your sins are now forgiven, as some of the more sacramental strains of Christianity would have it. "For" sounds like "for the sake of" or even "so that you might possess ..." Is that consistent with the rest of John's work, or even Jesus' proclamation, death, and resurrection?

To complicate things even more, I noticed something else. I was tempted to just write off this strange phrase. But then I found that this same phrasing occurs exactly one more time. It is also in Luke, in the very last chapter of the gospel. Jesus says to his disciples that "it is written that the Christ should suffer and on the third day rise from the dead, and that repentance and forgiveness of sins should be proclaimed in his name to all nations, beginning from Jerusalem" (24:46-47). Again, in Greek this 'and' is *eis* usually translated 'into.' So this phrase—"repentance into the forgiveness of sins"—bookends Jesus' proclamation. In Luke 24 the little preposition *eis* is translated in the ESV as a simple conjunction, "and." This implies that these two topics of repentance and forgiveness are part of the same bundle. But it says little or nothing about the relationship between the two. Yet in Luke 24, this verse lies at the heart of Jesus' definition of the church's proclamation. In other words, this is important. The other thing to note here is that in Luke 24, Jesus doesn't specifically mention baptism but he does include repentance. For the early church these two—baptism and repentance—were inextricably linked. Baptism came to include more: new birth, commissioning, bestowing of a new identity, renaming. But repentance, the act of turning away from the old life and receiving a new life, is right at the heart of it all. It is turning from an old way of life in bondage to the things of the world. It is a turning toward Jesus, toward the abundant life he gives.

What would happen if we translated that little preposition in its most common way—"into"?

Repentance *into* the forgiveness of sins. Hm. Sounds a little like forgiveness is a country where we are called to live, and repentance is the port of entry. Or forgiveness is the house, and repentance is the front door.

When you start thinking about forgiveness in this way, there is so much to say. Forgiveness is an enormous topic in scripture. Note that Adam and Eve are not taught how not to sin, but rather are given garments of skins. Skins require death and shedding of blood. In effect, these clothes cover their shame. In a sense the clothes symbolize forgiveness (see Genesis 3:21). God certainly does not take sin lightly, and neither should we. But God seems much more concerned to take away the power of sin that alienates us from one another and from God. This is exactly what forgiveness does. "Though your sins be as scarlet, they shall be white as snow," God says through Isaiah. Forgiveness, both from God to us and from us to each other, is a huge priority for God. Perhaps his plan is to create a community in which forgiveness is immediate and potent so that sin has no power to separate. When Peter asks Jesus how many times he must forgive, Jesus multiplies his answer and blows poor Peter right out of the water (see Matthew 18:21).

Is it true that God wants us to live in the forgiveness of sins like living in a beautiful, welcoming home? If so, our obsessive focus on not sinning (and on judging others who we catch sinning) might be diverting us from what God intends.

Note that Paul walks right up to this line in Romans 5, to the extent that at the outset of Romans 6 he has to anticipate the objection of his readers (much like as I write this I am concerned to anticipate the objections of my own readers). Paul writes, "Shall we go on sinning so that God's grace may abound? By no means!" Like Paul, I am not excusing sin. Absolutely not. But like Paul, I want to understand God's agenda and his priorities. As Paul goes on to say, as much as I wish sin was not present in my life, I seem unable to exorcise it (see Romans 7). The solution? Accept God's solution. "There is therefore now no condemnation for those who are in Christ Jesus" (Romans 8:1). It's almost as if the whole argument of Paul in Romans 5-8 is that rather than living in a strict moralistic, sin-preventing system, we should live in and by God's grace and mercy. God wants us to fully know his unlimited mercy and the cost of our forgiveness at the cross. Paul goes on to flesh out the forgiveness of sin and its implications in remarkable terms in the rest of Romans 8.

Repentance *into* the forgiveness of sins. Both in Luke 3 and in Luke 24, this idea is tied to the witness of the prophets and the entire Old Testament. Maybe this has been what God is up to all along.

Questions to think about:
1. Do you remember your own baptism, or do you know stories about it? What do you know?
2. What does the word "repentance" feel like to you? Is it a positive or negative word? Why?
3. Why do you suppose it is so difficult to prevent people (ourselves or others) from sinning?
4. How do you react to the picture of living in the forgiveness of sins like a country or a home?

Luke 3:7-17

An analyst of the poet Gerard Manley Hopkins described a cycle that repeated many times in Hopkins' life by using three terms: Encagement, Naturation, and Grace.

Encagement described the depressive phases all too common to Hopkins. He literally felt imprisoned, even at times suicidal. His poem "Carrion Comfort" is probably the strongest example of this extreme negative emotion and the self-assessment of his situation that went with it. There were a lot of reasons for these emotions; there were difficult things in Hopkins' life, especially in the area of personal relationships, that drove him to despair.

Hopkins turned to the natural world for some solace and the seedlings of hope. "Naturation" was the analyst's word to describe how Hopkins looked into the natural world—trees, birds, seasons, more—to find some comfort in the face of depression. You can trace in his poems the movement from despair upward toward a kind of hope. "Spring and Fall: To a young child" is a good example of the earlier kind, and "Pied Beauty" is perhaps typical of the later ones.

Grace describes what Hopkins was like at his spiritual and emotional best. He encountered the green, growing world and was eventually pried out of his own sinkholes of despair. Hopkins speaks in glowing terms of the beauty and sovereignty of God in Jesus Christ that shapes and forms his entire worldview. Hopkins in these stages could write paeans of praise like "The Windhover: To Christ our Lord" and many others. These poems are nothing short of delightful, both conceptually and in his inimitable use of language.

Why dig into Hopkins in this section of Luke?

The Jewish people were very much caught in something like "encagement" at this point in their history. For four hundred years they had longed for God to speak to them, but no prophet had arisen. They had longed for the completion of their Babylonian exile, and a return not only to their land (which had happened long before) but for God to take up residence in the temple at the heart of Jerusalem. They had tried, through their own efforts, to take up the mantle of being God's people. The best example of their efforts is the Maccabean revolt nearly two hundred years before. That episode resulted in a brief period of Jewish independence and even sovereignty. However, the resulting Hasmonean dynasty became corrupt and was finally defeated and occupied by Rome. So when John appears in the wilderness, the people have been living discouraged, defeated, depressed, dejected for generations.

How many of us live parallel struggles? We have grand hopes but we don't see God moving to fulfill what we think he's promised. We start to doubt his word. Sometimes we even doubt his goodness and his faithfulness. It is easy at such times to drift toward a jaded, agnostic cynicism. Either that or we fall prey to self-centered theologies that promise us prosperity and provide ways to manipulate God through our religious practices. These cheap theologies tell us that if we just have enough faith and tithe faithfully enough (or whatever the obedience du jour happens to be) God will do what we want. We regain the illusion of control. But controlling God is always an illusion.

We never get to control God's timelines. The life of faith is always a balancing act between learning patience and crying out "How long, O Lord?" But the fact that God doesn't operate according to my calendar doesn't mean he is unfaithful or has forgotten his promises. Far from it.

The Jewish people experienced a kind of "naturation" in John's preaching. They came out of the cities to the edge of the wilderness, out to the Jordan valley. Like Minnesotans migrating to the North Shore of Lake Superior, they went to the place of beauty and abundance, and the encounter with God's created world was refreshing. I sat in my recliner this morning for a while reflecting on my own context here on the shores of George Lake and what a healing place these seventy acres of natural beauty have become for me. I watch the fawns and their mothers, the rabbits and the woodchucks and the great blue heron that roosts in the willow tree along the edge of the bay, the beaver that has found something he really likes just off our north dock. All of these are balm to my encaged heart, and they turn me bit by bit toward the faithfulness of God.

John's preaching might not sound much like "good news" to us, but it is. John reminds the people that behavior is important, that turning away from their self-centered agendas (including the theologies of prosperity) makes room in them for God to work. In response to John's proclamation, the Jewish people begin to discover a revival of integrity. This is not the self-centered, controlling morality of the Pharisees. Rather it is a desire to align themselves with God who, John says, is up to something.

And that is the core of John's message. He points beyond himself to the One who is coming. Authentic revival will only happen if God moves. John says that God is about to move. Pay attention! The Messiah is standing among us right now! The inbreaking of God's action is right around the corner. When Jesus arrives, the surprise will be that he comes not with vengeance (though there will be judgment for those who insist on their own way) but rather with Grace. A different man named John would write about Jesus a few years later: "The Word became flesh and dwelt among us, full of grace and truth. And we beheld his glory, glory as the only son of a father." John the Baptist tells the people that God is moving, and their weary hearts will be healed when he acts.

Just at that moment, Jesus begins to make his way to the river bank.

Questions to think about:
1. Have you ever felt like you were caged? What was it like?
2. Is getting into the natural world a helpful, healing thing for you? Why / why not?

3. What might it feel like to be desperately hungry for God's Word?
4. Do you have a sense of God being on the move in your life? Why / why not?

Luke 3:18-22

A few years ago I read about a movement somewhere along the church's history that claimed God's plan was to have two surpassingly great prophets—John the Baptist and Jesus—and that Herod screwed up God's plan by having John killed. According to this theory, God's intention was that Jesus and John would have worked together to create a great partnership. They would function as a double Messiah, more or less.

To be clear, I totally reject this view, primarily because it flies in the face of everything the Bible has to say about both John and Jesus. John is incredibly important and has a critical role to play. The Bible is consistent in naming him as the archetypal prophet who will prepare the way for the Messiah's coming. This is why all the "Elijah" associations are so critically important when the New Testament describes John the Baptist. Faithful Jewish people in the first century knew their Bibles, and they held Malachi 3:1-5 and Malachi 4:5-6 constantly in mind. These passages tell how God will send his messenger, Elijah, to prepare the way.

Herod does not, in fact, circumvent God's plan, but his evil action in arresting and murdering John plays right into

God's hand. John was completely submitted to God, completely eager to do his will. No doubt John would have chosen a different fate for himself, but in the end his unpleasant end serves to highlight the singularity of Jesus. And John understood this. "He must increase, but I must decrease," John said even before his arrest (see John 3:30).

The biblical text consistently highlights Jesus as the unique agent of God's design. This is the heart of the theme that arises in the gospels naming Jesus as God's one-of-a-kind Son. "You are my beloved Son; with you I am well pleased." In Matthew the voice speaks to the bystanders. In John's gospel it is John the baptist himself speaking to the crowd, bearing witness to Jesus' identity. In Mark and Luke, God's voice speaks to Jesus himself, affirming Jesus' identity and calling. It is tantalizing to wonder just how much Jesus knew about these things before his baptism, but it seems clear at least that after his baptism he had a much clearer sense about himself. This makes his temptation (which we'll get to next section) that much more poignant.

"You are my beloved Son; in you I am well pleased." The book of Hebrews launches from this point into testimony about the surpassing supremacy of Jesus. It is an amazing declaration (see Hebrews 1:1-3).

Have you ever heard a parent speak words like this to you? Can you imagine what it would be to have an earthly father who spoke words like this? You are my beloved son (or daughter); in you I am well pleased. This is a parental blessing that is all too rare. What a powerful thing it is to have the privilege of pronouncing favor! I know a father who has struggled with his young adult daughter's feelings of shame and inadequacy, and he wonders how to love her well. Yet he continually reverts to evaluating her actions. "You did this really well," he says. "Now if you would just ..." This is judgment, analysis, criticism, evaluation. It is not blessing.

God speaks not in response to our actions or inaction; God speaks out of his own initiative, out of his own love. "You are my beloved," he says. "In you I am well pleased." God may very well go on to tell us many things he loves about us, and that, too, is a blessing. But his love begins with his own affection for us. It starts with the identity he has given us as a gift. God never loves in response to our worthiness. We live out that identity God has designed for us, in response to his initiative of love for us. Late in his life the apostle John would write, "We love because he first loved us." God always makes the first move.

It disturbs us, of course, that God's love for John might well look like letting him be beheaded by Herod. Herod's actions are the farthest thing from God's character. He is weak and selfish and afraid of people's opinions. He becomes violent and capricious. We will get to the story of John's death later. Here, however, Luke wants us to see the contrast. John is the opening act; Jesus is the main event. John is the prophet; Jesus is the Messiah. John is the forerunner, Jesus is the Son of God. God has spent all of history setting up this moment, as Jesus' genealogy makes clear. We'll head there next time.

Questions to think about:
1. Can you remember your parents blessing you in some way? What was that like?
2. What might it feel like to hear God say, "You are my beloved son / daughter; in you I am well pleased"?
3. What would it mean for us to say (like John) that Jesus must increase, but we must decrease?
4. How has God taken the initiative to show his love for you in the last few days or weeks?

Luke 3:23-38

There's an ad I've been hearing a lot lately for a DNA analysis service. The ad says that by getting your DNA analysis you can find out who you are and where you come from. In our post-Enlightenment world, this seems like a rational statement. In the pre-Enlightenment world, it would have seemed laughable. How will a chemical analysis of your chromosomal makeup tell you anything about who you are or where you come from?

Your DNA might tell you whether you're prone to heart disease or type 1 diabetes, and those are important questions. It might tell you about the human migrations that shaped your ancestry, and that's interesting. But we don't gain a sense of who we are and where we come from through chemistry; we get these things through the relationships that shape us, the stories we tell ourselves, and the names we are given.

This is why the genealogies are included in both Matthew and Luke, and this is why they're important. Both Matthew and Luke, in very different ways, use the genealogies of Jesus to make statements about him, about the people of Israel, and about us. Matthew uses the genealogy in Matthew 1 to tie Jesus intimately into the history of Israel. Through this genealogy Matthew highlights both the noble calling of the descendants of Abraham and their ongoing patterns of sin, bigotry, violence, and selfishness. Matthew shows Jesus as the fulfillment of God's promises to Abraham, especially the promise in Genesis 12 that all the nations of the earth would be blessed through Abraham's descendants.

Luke, on the other hand, is telling a different story. He is less concerned about Israel's history and calling and more concerned about Jesus coming for all humanity, coming as a light to all nations. Remember that Luke's primary audience is a non-Jewish man, a Roman official, and Luke deftly tells Jesus' story through his genealogy to include Theophilus. While Matthew traces Jesus' ancestry back to Abraham, Luke carefully goes back even further to Adam, and then to God. Jesus has come for all people. This is one of Luke's primary themes throughout the gospel.

If you read them, you'll find that Matthew and Luke have very different genealogies for Jesus. In fact, Matthew traces Jesus' ancestry through David's son Solomon, down the royal line through the exile in Babylon. Very likely this was Joseph's lineage, as Matthew says he was "of the house and line of David." The version in Luke is quite different, however. Many scholars believe, given the fact that Luke obviously used Mary as a significant source for his gospel, that this list, tracing back through David's son Nathan, was Mary's own ancestry. Luke acknowledges right at the beginning of the genealogy that Jesus was not biologically Joseph's son, but that makes sense if he's using Mary's genealogy here.

Luke uses the genealogy to focus on archetypes, among other things. Luke had been a companion of Paul, and no doubt would have heard and read in Paul's teaching this idea of archetypes that was so familiar to Paul. This is not a way of thinking that we commonly use, so it may seem foreign and unimportant to us. Contrast the way Paul uses Adam and Christ in the last part of Romans 5, for example, and you might begin to see how critical this way of thinking was to Paul. It was well understood in the ancient world that archetypes were critically important to understanding one's self. In our world, we might begin to get the significance of this if we wrapped together our passion for a favorite sports team, our Myers-Briggs type assessment, Strengthsfinders analysis, favorite nickname bestowed by someone we love, and a movie character we deeply identify with. If you take all the impact of all those categories added together in your life, you may begin to get at what it means to have an archetypal identification with a person. This and much more is what Paul is up to in Romans 5 as he talks about being "in Adam" or "in Christ." Paul uses this same tool in Galatians as he talks about Hagar and Sarah and contrasts them. Jesus used archetypal language as well, and frequently we fail to understand the Bible at these points because we are so conditioned to post-Enlightenment ways of viewing truth and meaning.

So Luke is telling us important things. Jesus is the "son of God" both because of his miraculous conception by the Holy Spirit, and also because he is descended down the line of all humanity from Adam. He identifies with God in his "incarnation" but he also identifies with us. He is the ultimate human being. It is this identification with us in our fallen humanity that leads Jesus to "fulfill all righteousness" by coming to be baptized in the Jordan River. It is this identification with us in our fallen humanity that leads Jesus into his mission to rescue us from our alienation and brokenness. And it is this stepping into the role of being the New Adam that brings Jesus squarely up against the forces that have kept the Old Adam in chains. Now Jesus will have to face the deep conflict created by his mission. He will be tempted by humanity's archenemy in the wilderness. That's where we're headed next.

Questions to think about:
1. Have you ever been given a name? A nickname, a pet name? What is it like to be named?
2. Do you make use of personality inventories? If so, how does knowing your type influence you?
3. How many generations back do you know your own genealogy? Is that important to you?
4. How might Theophilus have understood from this genealogy that Jesus came for him?

Luke 4:1-13

Books have been written about these few verses, with good reason. I remember many years ago being part of a men's group reading Donald Kraybill's *The Upside-Down Kingdom* that used these temptation stories as a way to get inside how Jesus turns this world's systems and expectations on their heads.

An older man whom I deeply respect talks about how Jesus' temptations address the three main spheres of life: economic (bread), political (kingdoms), and religious (temple). By refusing Satan's enticements, Jesus shows his holiness and lordship over all the main realms of human life.

There's lots here to ponder.

One of the things I've wondered about in this story over the years is the timing of it. The temptation comes hard on the heels of Jesus' baptism and God's pronouncement that "you are my beloved Son in whom I am well pleased." Though there's no definitive way to answer this, I've wondered many times what was going on for Jesus in this moment. Did Jesus at his baptism receive a full sense of his own identity and his mission? I've come to believe this is true. No doubt (especially given Luke's retelling of the twelve-year-old Jesus in the temple) Jesus prior to his baptism had an idea of his special relationship with God the Father. He had probably heard Mary's stories of his miraculous conception and birth. It is possible, even likely, that it is in his baptism Jesus receives the fullness of his identity and mission from the Father through the Spirit that descends on him.

One of the strongest arguments in favor of this idea is that when Satan addresses Jesus and says "If you are the Son of God..." the Greek grammar doesn't imply doubt. In fact, it's not going too far to translate Satan's suggestions as "*Since* you are the Son of God..." And that makes me think Jesus has just learned the fullness of his own identity, and probably the trajectory of his mission that will lead to the cross. It's a lot to take in, and it makes sense that in that moment, Satan would step up with easier, less painful alternatives. Since you are the Son of God, why not use a little of your power to feed your body? Since you are the Son of God, why not receive these kingdoms from me rather than walk this hard road to the cross? Since you are the Son of God, why not wow the Jewish people with a miraculous sign that will win you a mass of followers from the outset?

Jesus has been named by the Father. He has been given the fullness of his God-given identity. He knows himself as the beloved one, the Son of God. What will he do in this new identity? Will he walk the hard road to the cross? Or is there an easier alternative? It must have been a heady temptation, given the frothing anticipation of Jesus' people for their Messiah. What they hoped for was very much in line with Satan's temptations. They wanted the charismatic political Messiah who would benefit them economically and socially. Jesus recognizes the dangerous, diabolical nature of the easy road Satan offers.

We are often tempted to make Jesus more divine than the biblical texts allow. The temptation story is one of the most important moments for us to recognize the full humanity of Jesus. If we don't, we will not receive the value of Jesus' example for ourselves. As the book of Hebrews states, Jesus was tempted in every way like we have, but was without sin.

So what about you? Have you been named? Such a name might be given by God, by parents, by those who love you. This is not just a name people can call across the parking lot. It is an identity, a deep sense of who you are. It gives a sense of your unique calling. And if you have this deep sense of yourself that has been bestowed on you, how will you pursue that unique mission, that one-of-a-kind contribution God has designed for you to accomplish in his good creation? There will always be wide gates and broad, paved pathways that beckon. There will be ways that offer the comfort of self-indulgence. The compromise of selling your soul to gain the world is a constant temptation. The people-pleasing choices that enhance your own status but don't really direct people to the character of God will always whisper in your ears.

In the end, that's what drives Jesus' rejection of Satan's careful biblical quotations. Jesus chooses to align himself with the Father's character, even though it might cost him discomfort, personal pain, and disapproval of the masses.

1. Where did your name come from? What does it mean?
2. What is it like to be tempted? Do you believe Jesus was honestly tempted by Satan's offers? Why / why not?
3. If Jesus just received the full knowledge of his mission at his baptism, what might he have been feeling as he absorbed this new information?
4. How does Jesus' mission, including rejecting the easy ways to popularity and going to the cross, reflect God the Father's heart?

Luke 4:14-30

You have to feel at least a little bad for the people of Nazareth. The trouble for them, as so often for us, is that they don't really want to know Jesus accurately. Knowing Jesus for who he is demands a great deal of us, and it leads us into uncomfortable territory.

The people of Nazareth wanted a few simple things. We miss a lot of what's happening in this passage because we don't understand the plight of small-town Jews in Galilee in the first century. They were caught in tides that threatened to wash away their traditional culture, and they could feel the ebb and flow every day. Nowhere was this more true than in Nazareth. The New Testament doesn't directly mention the larger city of Sepphoris just up the road. Sepphoris was a culturally Greek city that had been founded by Rome. The city provided a major engine to drive the local economy. Traditional Jews living in Nazareth felt overshadowed by the Greek culture and economy a short walk up the road. Everything that happens in the scene Luke here is overshadowed by the cultural tensions in Nazareth.

Jesus was becoming famous, and the people of Nazareth wanted to share in the glory of a hometown boy made good. Second, they wanted to maintain their own views about who God was and what he was up to. Third, they wanted to keep their illusions about themselves and their circumstances. Jesus' words and actions here in his hometown fly in the face of all those desires. No wonder by the end of the story they want to kill him.

They want to share in the glory of a hometown boy made good: Luke makes clear that Jesus has been preaching throughout Galilee, and we can assume that his preaching, as later, included healing people, casting out demons, and all the rest. His reputation grew. So the people of Nazareth were very much like the people of a small town whose local athlete makes it big in the pros. Reporters come around looking for the "I knew him when" story. The city fathers put up a "home of..." billboard on the highway coming into town. Sportscasters love to allude to the small town, small school, normal hometown stories. In a way, all this serves to validate the small town itself, along with all its residents. See? Our town must be okay. Look at the great athlete who grew up here! Our small lives are not mean and meaningless. (No one else is saying their lives are meaningless, btw.) In similar fashion, Jesus' homecoming could have been a pep rally for the local kid. That's what's going on in verses 16-22. Jesus has already dropped the bomb (more on that in a minute) but the delighted people of Nazareth haven't even heard the sermon, they're so preoccupied with this second-degree brush with fame. Throughout his ministry, Jesus has zero patience for those who are hungry to see something miraculous to fuel their self-focused gossip. Nazareth is just the first of many times Jesus will refuse to participate in this agenda. It is the same refusal that Jesus has just pronounced to Satan three times over. He refuses to use his connection with God to serve his own desires. He will not compromise his identity in God's sight to gain worshipers. He will not use the spectacular to fuel his movement. Jesus makes clear: when the miraculous occurs, it serves a greater purpose than our own fascination. The people of Nazareth, quiet bedroom community of the much larger Greek-culture driven city of Sepphoris four miles away, are looking for a miracle to legitimize their pride. Jesus, the wildly successful prophet who was burning up the wires in Galilee, could validate them by coming home and saying, "I owe it all to these people and this little town," but he doesn't.

In short, they wanted to keep their illusions about who God was and what he was up to. They were certain God was Jewish and he wanted the Jews to isolate themselves in their perceived superiority. They were the faithful people, after all. They were the chosen ones, and God would vindicate their status and their isolationism. The Greek theater and gymnasium in Sepphoris might drive their local economy. It might give them good jobs (perhaps Joseph

and even Jesus had served in the construction projects
that were going on in this era in Sepphoris). They might
have to speak Greek in the marketplaces even though they
spoke Aramaic at home and read the scriptures in Hebrew
at the synagogue. But in the long run, they knew God
would destroy those pagans and their anti-God culture.
They dearly loved the passage Jesus chose to read from
the prophet Isaiah, and they knew it well. The trouble is,
Jesus stopped reading too soon. He quit before he got to
the good part, the part they were waiting to see fulfilled. He
quit reading before he got to the part about God vindicating
the Jews and making the pagans come and serve them.
And then he had the gall to say that this scripture, this
passage that makes the Jews dream of better days to
come, has already been fulfilled. What?!

They want to keep their illusions about themselves and
their calling. It is so often tempting for us to live on our
fantasies and delusions. We have dreams about the future
and what it might mean, and it's easy to get caught on the
hamster wheel of imagination. We use fantasy about the
future to escape the present. But the fact is, if the fantasy
is in fact a God-given vision, the present is the time to be
working toward its fulfillment. Every God-given vision about
the future requires that we grow in our own capacity to
receive it. Oswald Chambers says that God gives us the
vision on the mountaintop, then he brings us into the valley
to beat us into shape to receive it. The people of Nazareth
have mistaken the vision, first of all. They believe it's a
self-centered vision about themselves being exalted and
(in Steinbeck's phrase) living off the fat of the land. God's
intention, instead, is that his chosen people should be a

kingdom of priests to call all nations into relationship with him. For a picture of what this is supposed to look like, read Psalm 96. Instead, the frustrated, oppressed people of Nazareth yearned for the day when aliens would tend their flocks and foreigners would do their field work (see Isaiah 61:5). God was on a mission to reach the world, but his missionary people had decided they'd rather have the world for household servants.

Jesus returns to his hometown and quotes a favorite scripture passage, then says that God is already doing the necessary work to bring it to fulfillment. Jesus focuses on the critical part of Isaiah 61, the part that defines his role. He is called to be the bearer of good news to the nations, to proclaim recovery of sight to the blind, to set the oppressed free, to tell people God looks on them with favor. This had, in fact, been the calling of the entire Jewish nation since long before Isaiah spoke those words hundreds of years before. This calling goes all the way back to Abraham in Genesis 12. Jesus focuses on his own role and steps up to fulfill God's calling to Israel. He exposes the self-centered attitudes of the people of Nazareth for the delusions they are. God is not primarily a God who wreaks vengeance on the nations, Jesus says. Instead God sends his best prophets to places like Sepphoris to reach those who don't know him. He loves the widow and the leper from other nations just like he loves the Jews. Don't you know your own history?

Rather than acknowledge God's call to them, the people of Nazareth rise up in anger to throw Jesus off the cliff. Their surge of wrath is well-known to anyone who has spoken biblical truth into a tradition-bound, insecure congregation or community. Jesus gets jostled a bit, but in the end he just walks away. Later he will tell his disciples that if the towns of Israel don't receive them and their message, they should shake the dust off their feet as they're leaving town. He is speaking out of his own painful experience. Jesus will spend his ministry calling his own people to a greater vision of their calling and identity. Most of them will miss it, as the church down through the centuries all too often misses exactly this same call. This theme will echo through Jesus' teaching. "Those who have ears, let them hear," Jesus says.

<u>Questions to think about:</u>
1. Have you ever felt defensive when you've heard someone criticize you or your community? What was that like?
2. Do you agree that a "prophet is without honor in his hometown"? Why / why not?
3. Reread the verses Jesus reads from Isaiah 61. What emotions would you use to describe Jesus' ministry, if this is what it will be like?
4. Have you ever had to "shake the dust off your feet"? What was that like?

Luke 4:31-37

This story of Jesus restoring a demon-possessed man in the synagogue provides a good opportunity to ponder two things: First, the craftsmanship of God, and second the timing of God.

In Galatians Paul writes that "when the fullness of time had come, God sent his Son, born of a woman, born under the law ..." (Galatians 4:4). That phrase, "the fullness of time" includes so much about God's craftsmanship. Over two thousand years, God carefully created a people with strands of meaning and deep, rich traditions. The Jewish culture in the first century was rich. It serves both as a platform for Jesus' saving work, and also as a framework to help us understand more completely who Jesus is and what he is about.

Elements in Luke 4 point to God's craftsmanship. A few examples: The existence of Galilee itself is a major factor. Galilee at this time was an area of dense Jewish settlement, so Jewish scriptures and culture were predominant there. But Galilee, unlike Jerusalem, also contained many non-Jewish elements (like Sepphoris in the previous section). So the Jewish culture that dominated Galilee was also tempered by interaction with elements of other cultures. Judea in the south, and more so Jerusalem, were much more wholly Jewish without as much influence from non-Jewish cultures. The fact that most of Jesus' ministry happens in Galilee, and that he was raised in this crossroads of cultures, cannot be overemphasized.

The fact that this story takes place in the synagogue is another example of God's craftsmanship. Prior to the Babylonian exile in 587 BC, Israelite worship took place almost exclusively in the temple in Jerusalem. Other worship did occur, and usually the Old Testament refers to this as worship that happens on the "high places." Such worship tended to be a syncretistic blend of the worship of Yahweh and other gods, and in various places the Old Testament either tolerates or condemns it. But with the Babylonian exile the Israelites found themselves cut off from the temple. They were forced to contemplate their generational idolatry and God's judgment. They became desperately concerned to have an appropriate way to worship in other lands. Out of this exile over time grew several elements that, combined, came to define the word "Jewish." Those elements include

- Written scriptures (which had existed at some level prior to the exile but played a minor role in Israelite religion),
- The role of rabbis (previously priests occupied the official leadership roles, and their service was tied directly to the temple), and
- The existence of synagogues–dedicated centers of worship wherever at least ten Jewish men were gathered. The synagogues (a Greek word that is roughly equivalent to the English word "congregation") sprouted up as Jewish people dispersed throughout the Near East. Synagogues provided the core of a system that enabled the Jews to maintain their culture while scattered in foreign lands. This scattered population became known as the Diaspora.

There is much more to say here about how God had brought elements of other cultures and religions to play. The Jewish belief in a God who is all powerful and all good but who is opposed by demonic forces, for example, had been influenced by this careful craftsmanship. Over centuries God crafted a rich worldview that had come into its own about the time Jesus arrives on the scene. But to do such a topic justice would require more paragraphs than we have space or time for here.

On to the second major theme, that of timing. I have often said (sometimes by faith in the face of my own frustration) that God has perfect timing. Of course this is what Paul is getting at in Galatians 4 in saying that the "fullness of time" had come. Often the easiest way to see God's timing is to look for intersections. What are the necessary elements that suddenly come together in a window of opportunity? There are several major strands that intersect for a few decades in the first century. To grossly oversimplify:

- Jewish monotheism: As stated above, the worldview of Jewish monotheism had really come into its own at this time. So many strands of cultural influence (Egyptian, Canaanite, Babylonian, Greek, and more) helped to shape the fullness of what began with Abraham and Moses. Their relationship with Yahweh by Jesus' time had grown into a rich cultural and religious system that permeated every aspect of Jewish life.

- Greek language and culture: Three and a half centuries before Jesus' ministry, Alexander the Great marched across the eastern Mediterranean (and beyond), evangelizing the world with Greek culture. He intentionally imposed Greek gymnasiums, theaters, and marketplaces. Above all he insisted on a simplified (*koine*) version of the

Greek language. Cultural ideas about beauty, meaning, ethics, excellence were all shaped by the legacy of Alexander. The New Testament emerges in the sharp intersection of this Greek culture with Jewish monotheism, and the dynamic explosion of Christianity is only possible because of the unifying factor of *koine* Greek. The world would not know such linguistic possibility again until the 20th century.

- A third major element in this question of timing is the *pax Romana*, the brutally enforced peace of Rome. Rome's iron fist required the ability to transport troops rapidly across the empire, and so roads and shipping were carefully constructed and jealously protected. (Eisenhower's vision of a military transportation network in the 1950's leading to the United States Interstate Highway system is a modern parallel.) Roman roads and the suppression of piracy allowing for safe travel throughout the Mediterranean created an opportunity for this fledgling Jesus-movement to grow and expand rapidly across the empire.

There is obviously so much more to say about these things, but it's important to note that this strange scene in a synagogue in Capernaum where Jesus restores a demon-possessed man happens in a much wider context. This carefully crafted, precisely timed moment, is no accident. It is an amazing demonstration of the craftsmanship and timing of God. God's chosen Messiah, at this specific moment in history, steps out in power and heals a demon-possessed man. The fact that this happened, and that Jesus' hearers understood it as they did, and that they communicated about it in a way that has come down to us, demonstrates the timing and craftsmanship of God.

What are the places in your own life that God has carefully assembled factors? Can you see that God has been at work, lovingly sculpting these different forces to bring you to the precise place where you find yourself today? Can you trust that God is working the timing in your own life, bringing the intersection of opportunities? Until he shows all his cards, it's hard to see what God is up to. Trust him. Let faith inform your frustration and believe that he has good plans. His fulfillment will be better than what you would plan for yourself. Like those in the first century who encountered Jesus, be ready. When the time comes to grab hold of what God is doing, you don't want to miss the moment. In the meantime, trust him.

Questions to think about:
1. What is the most surprising thing you've ever seen in a church service?
2. How comfortable are you pondering the great movements of history and how they affect what we read about in the Bible?
3. How do you suppose the healed man felt about Jesus? What about others who witnessed this event?
4. Is this an effective way for Jesus' ministry to gain momentum? Why / why not?

Luke 4:38-41

These few verses highlight one of the most consistent and important aspects of Jesus' ministry: he healed people. Even the most agnostic of historians acknowledge that Jesus must have had some kind of gift of healing, or at least a reputation as such. Simon's mother-in-law and the multitudes who come are just the first of so many in the gospels who will experience physical, spiritual, emotional, relational restoration at Jesus' touch.

Today we have eliminated much of our need for wandering healers. We possess miraculous medical technology that eliminates many diseases, heals wounds, and curbs the discomfort of conditions we cannot ultimately heal. Life expectancy has risen consistently as a result of the incredible medical discoveries that we now take for granted. Case in point, I'm a type one diabetic, diagnosed shortly before I turned eight years old. A hundred years ago I might have endured into my teens, but no more than that. I've taken insulin by injections and later by a pump for more than four decades, and today I live a remarkably normal, physically robust life. My life is good and so full and the affect of my diabetes on my daily life is minor. I thank God for my good health and all the blessings I enjoy because of it, and I recognize that part of what I have to be thankful for is the advancement of medical technology.

At the same time, I recognize that this is still, in spite of insulin pumps and all the other medical advancements, a broken world. In the first century, a sense of hopelessness and alienation was driven significantly, among other things, by physical diseases that were beyond cure. Today our evidence of brokenness looks a little different. Yes, we enjoy better physical health. But we are still a broken people. In many cases we have traded physical maladies for emotional, relational and spiritual ones.

In some cases our brokenness is a byproduct of the same technological advances that make us healthier. While CAT scans, contact lenses and cold medicines help us physically, similar technologies have made us more mobile, even transient. One of the byproducts of technology is an increasing loneliness that afflicts us like a plague. The loneliness that in part results from our transience and our ability to self-medicate with too much screen time leads us down the road toward an epidemic of anxiety, depression, and despair.

Perhaps we need to rediscover Jesus as the healer for these ills. While our individualism and post-Enlightenment thinking predisposes us to loneliness, Jesus calls us not only into relationship with himself but into relationship with one another. Jesus' followers are designed to live in community. Every example of people coming to faith in Jesus in the New Testament also includes a nod toward an ongoing community that will become like a new family to the believer. Like any family, these relationships in the Jesus-following community will not be perfect. But they will provide a healthy system in which life can be lived in all its God-intended abundance.

One of the visions that gives me hope for the church in a post-Christendom context is that of home-sized communities. Call them house churches or what have you. They build a spiritual, emotional, relational family around each individual. When I have seen the church function like this I have also seen that every form of brokenness has opportunity to be healed in that context. Not everyone wants to be made well, of course, and not every disease is healed. Yet Jesus presents himself in these relational contexts as our healer, as the restorer of wholeness and abundant life. Such health is as much a gift today as seeing a lame man rise and walk in the first century.

Questions to think about:
1. Do you believe technology is more of a blessing for us than a curse? Explain.
2. What might it have been like for people in Jesus' day to experience him as healer?
3. Have you ever experienced any kind of healing, or witnessed it? What was that like?
4. How can Jesus' followers help bring healing to those who experience loneliness, anxiety, or depression?

Luke 4:42-44

"And when it was day he departed and went into a desolate place." Over and over again we see Jesus seeking desolate places. This is one of the hardest aspects of his life for us to imitate.

We do not suffer (both in the sense of "endure" and in the sense of being miserable in the enduring) desolation well. We cheat ourselves of the fullness of all God wants for us because we fill our time with entertainment and avoid desolation at all costs. And when, in the wisdom of God, we are thrust into desolation, we usually hate it. Instead of growing in it, we strive to end it as soon as possible.

Have you ever said, "I need a vacation to recover from my vacation"? Have you ever felt like you were trying to work to 110% of your capacity? Strange as it may seem to us, periodic desolation is an important part of the cure.

Understand, life needs many things to be what Jesus called "abundant," and he himself is at the center of such a life. Healthy community, meaningful work, loving intimacy, healing vulnerability, diverting entertainment, enlightening conversation, stretching silence: all these things are necessary for the abundant life. As much as I don't like it, I think that the experience of periodic desolation needs to be on that list as well.

There are two categories of desolation, at least in my mind. Voluntary desolations are those we schedule for ourselves. These might look like vacations but they are not full of amusements or tourist attractions; rather they are a chance to unplug from the world and reconnect to God, often in the context of nature. There's something hardwired in us to rediscover ourselves by brushing up against the wilderness. I've done a couple solo trips to the Boundary Waters in northern Minnesota and these have provided voluntary desolation for me. In some ways it has been uncomfortable, without a doubt. By definition these trips have taken me off the grid, away from cell phones and emails and social media. Very often, God has spoken in significant ways in that context, whether I'm alone or with others. I've learned to structure the hard work of traveling by canoe interspersed with days in camp. Quiet times to contemplate the lake and the fire and the breeze and sometimes the mosquitos and the rain are a beginning. It's a voluntary desolation, and I'm always better for it.

Involuntary desolations are the ones we desperately want to avoid. These are the ones that twist our insides to the breaking point. Grief at the loss of a loved one, the brokenness of a relationship, the aftermath of a divorce, physical illness or emotional breakdowns, seasons of burnout—all of these and more bring us to a kind of involuntary desolation. Sometimes we end up in these involuntary desolations because we have refused to hear God's call into voluntary desolation.

Terry Walling has done some excellent work on how the experience of being "stuck" is used by God to provide transitions. Some of what he describes sounds a lot like God using both voluntary and involuntary desolation to shape, form, and redirect us. One of Terry's most significant themes is that there are transitions that nearly everyone goes through at specific stages in life. These include entering young adulthood and discerning your calling; moving toward significance in adulthood as you discern your unique contribution; and entering into a kind of blessed convergence nearer the end of life. Each of these transitions presents us with a kind of crisis. We endure a sense of desolation, a feeling of being stuck. God is at work in huge ways in each of these major transitions, and in the lesser ones we experience.

Jesus invites us into periodic voluntary desolation. If you are in a desolate place as you read this, know that God is there with you. Swallow the lump in your throat and know that Jesus has been there before you. He will not leave you alone. He is working for your good in all this, even though it might be desperately hard. The discomfort will be worth it. In Jesus' own life in these verses, his time of suffering desolation leads to a major transition. He moves from focusing on Galilee to preaching in the villages of Judea. As you deal with the desolate hours, know that God is doing his good work. Though it might seem right now like everything is stuck, there will come a moment when God moves you out of the transition and into a new stage. As Tom Petty sang, "the waiting is the hardest part." But God is faithful.

Questions to think about:
1. What is it like for you to be "off the grid"? How often do you set aside time for rest?
2. What emotions do you associate with the word "desolate"?
3. How do you think God works in our desolate times, even in times of grief and brokenness? Have you seen him work in this way?
4. How might you follow Jesus example of seeking out desolate places in your life?

Luke 5:1-11

It's fascinating to imagine this event from Peter's perspective. You're cleaning things up after a long, discouraging night of fishing with your partners. You're a little frustrated and a little worried, because if there are no fish there's no income. You work with the others to meticulously clean your equipment and deep down you're racking your brains to figure out what you should be doing different next time. A hubbub down the shoreline begins to intrude into your thoughts. There's a crowd, and it's coming this way. Jesus emerges and, presumptuous, steps right into your boat! Then he asks you to push him out a few feet into the water, as the unruly crowd won't even give him a few feet of space. So you, maybe grumbling a bit under your breath, get into the boat. Jesus sits down, like any sensible person does in a boat, but also like a rabbi preparing to teach. And you're stuck. You sit there listening to his teaching, as long as he cares to go on. You're a captive audience. When Jesus finally finishes his teaching, he starts giving you fishing advice, and it's contrary to what you know to be good fishing practice. You don't find fish in deep water, and the nets won't enclose them that way! But you don't want to look impious or rude to the Rabbi, so after a couple objections you play along. And suddenly a barren night's work becomes boat-filling fruitful. At that point, with nets at their tearing point and fish flopping all over your feet and the gunwales getting dangerously close to the water, you realize that this teacher is more than you imagined. God is up to something here, and you're invited right into the middle of it. Suddenly Peter sees, really sees, Jesus, and he falls to his knees there in the pile of fish. Jesus recognizes a heart ready to receive his call, and he tells Peter he'll be fishing for people from now on.

A couple observations. First, Jesus very often shows up in your work. He often shows up in that moment when your good, meaningful work has become frustrating, when it feels unproductive and barren. He takes the tools of your work and he turns them just a little to use them for his purposes. And he invites you along. You find yourself in that moment focused in a new way on Jesus, and your understanding of him and his purposes grows.

Second, Peter narrowly missed a great danger. He could have been so stuck in his own frustration and fear that he missed an invitation to a greater life. Simply put, Peter could have said, "No." When Jesus invites us to step out into something larger than what we've known in the past, very often our vision is too small and we completely miss the opportunity. Peter complains, he objects, but he is in the end obedient to Jesus. Peter obeys both in the initial, small thing of pushing his boat out as Jesus requests, and then in the call to leave his nets. Not just the nets themselves, but also all they represented. Peter was a fisherman; his nets represented income, security, a niche in the local community, even family. Peter follows Jesus into a greater adventure.

Third, this is not the first time Peter's been close to Jesus. Remember, Jesus previously healed Peter's mother-in-law from a fever. Jesus doesn't expect you out of the blue to drop everything. Can you look back and see how he has prepared you? He has planted his love and his identity and his power in your life. Can you see where the seeds of this call have been dropped into you earlier so that when the call comes, you've been prepared?

Finally, Jesus speaks Peter's language. The great move of Jesus' incarnation is what theologians call "kenosis." It means "emptying" (see Philippians 2) and it's what God the Son, 2nd person of the Trinity, did to become Jesus of Nazareth, a human being who could sit in Peter's boat. In a tiny way, we see Jesus do this same kind of stepping down again and again: he frames himself and his call to Peter in terms Peter can understand. He doesn't sit down and give Peter a theology class there on the shore; instead he reduces a life-transformation down to terms Peter can receive. "From now on you will fish for people." Jesus knows that Peter will expand into greater truth, greater understanding, as he follows. Jesus does the very same thing with us.

Questions to think about:
1. What is your most / least favorite thing about work?
2. What excuses could Peter have given for refusing Jesus' request?
3. How might the story be different if Peter still didn't catch any fish?
4. How might Jesus want to use you in your work?

Luke 5:12-26

These two accounts of Jesus healing (first a leper, second a paralytic) highlight the contrast between Jesus and the cultural practices and authorities of the Jewish religion of the time. In a wider sense, they contrast Jesus over against any human systems and efforts. These contrasts center around issues of will, authority, and perception. And don't miss that in the hinge between the two stories, Luke reminds us that Jesus seeking desolate places was not just a one-time thing, but an important pattern for him.

The question of will dominates the healing of the leper. What is God's will for those who are broken? Jesus clearly states, then acts on the statement, that his will is wholeness. Have you ever wondered whether God has good intentions toward you? Have you ever wondered if God is really the mean kid who picks the wings off flies, and you're now stuck in the windowsill, crawling around wishing you could fly? Jesus says no. He *wills* that you should be healed, whole, free, flying. (I realize that in this metaphor we are houseflies, but this gets at the power and authority dynamics, so it's probably okay.) God wills your healing, your wholeness, your joy. This is radically different from saying God simply wants you to be happy. That shallow heresy dominates so many people's thinking. The joy God desires for you is partnered with strength. We see this partnership time and time again in Jesus' own life. Strength comes through enduring difficulty (see Romans 5) and God longs for his beloved children to grow strong, whole, and joyful. He will not always pad the sharp corners or prevent the consequences of their choices. Instead he will use adversity and difficulty. He has authority over these things as well.

That is the upshot of the fascinating account of the paralytic brought to Jesus through the roof of a house. There is a lot to say about this story, but a few comments will have to suffice here. First, notice that it is the gaggle of religious leaders and teachers crowded around Jesus that prevents the paralytic from gaining access. How often do religious people clump together and prevent the good news of Jesus from being scattered into the world like salt and light are supposed to be scattered? There is an indictment here of formalized religious systems that will build throughout the following stories. (More on this when we talk about wine & wineskins in 5:37-39.)

Not only do the religious leaders impede the man's access to Jesus in a physical sense, but they want to stand in the way of Jesus' pronouncement of forgiveness. Without a doubt some of them would have opposed the healing itself, as we see elsewhere in the gospels. Jesus responds by getting to the heart of the matter: His own authority. He has authority to pronounce forgiveness of sins AND to heal the paralytic and make him whole.

The authority to forgive is one that is too often missed. This is an incredibly significant action on Jesus' part, and the Jewish religious leaders understood its implications. Assuming that the paralytic had not met Jesus before, and that he had done nothing directly against Jesus that required forgiveness, Jesus cannot possibly pronounce forgiveness to him. Only an injured party can pronounce forgiveness. The exception, of course, is that God can forgive, because all sin injures God. So the only way Jesus can say with anything resembling truth, "Your sins are forgiven" is if he in fact is God in some sense, or at the very least speaks with authority directly from God.

At the heart of it, Jesus reveals here the tension that will eventually get him crucified: He stands opposed to the power structures and authority structures by which sinful humanity governs itself. If he is truly the king of the kingdom of God, then the religious and political leaders have no ultimate claim. At best they have a penultimate claim, exercising very limited authority because God has dispensed it to them in a measured way. (This is in fact a key element of Jesus' conversation with Pontius Pilate in John's gospel.)

The final statement of the crowd—"We have seen extraordinary things today"–is telling because we too easily get accustomed to this world's "ordinary." We get accustomed to corrupt rulers and self-important systems that prevent people from really experiencing the wholeness God wills for his people. We get accustomed to settling for mediocrity and brokenness in our own lives. The life of the kingdom of God is not for weaklings or cowards, a la "The Secret Life of Walter Mitty." In the written version, Walter lived with delusions and fantasies that helped him avoid the realities of his situation. Instead, we are called to see the pain and brokenness inherent in ourselves and in this world, then confidently turn to Jesus because we know both his will and his authority. To us and through us, he brings healing, wholeness, joy, and strength.

Questions to think about:
1. What is the greatest number of people you've ever had in your home? How crowded was it?
2. What does it mean that God's will is healing and wholeness? Why is there still so much hurt in the world?
3. How is Jesus forgiving the man's sins connected to Jesus healing him, according to Luke?
4. What is it like to forgive someone? Are there people who have injured you whom you need to forgive?

Luke 5:27-39

Though the story of Jesus eating with Levi and the tax collectors and sinners is usually separated from Jesus' words about wine and wineskins, the two belong together. When Jesus chooses to eat with the tax collectors and sinners, when he calls a tax collector to be one of the Twelve, he is not just living out some sort of parable that will offend and expose the religious leaders. Rather, Jesus is living by a completely different set of standards that he called "the kingdom of God." Under the rules of that kingdom, the sinners are the right people to dine with. Levi is the right person to call to follow. Jesus is simply living out his kingship. The religious leaders judge *themselves* by questioning and opposing him. (According to the New Testament, we are judged by how we respond to Jesus.)

Occasionally you see this same kind of event in major leadership transitions. A congregation that is deeply chained to its tradition gets a new leader who lives according to kingdom principles and seeks to advance a mission for the church that reflects God's character. In doing so, the leader enacts sweeping change. The power blocs (the matriarchs and patriarchs of the congregation) question and oppose. And, if the leader accurately reflects God's character, those power blocs judge themselves in the opposing. Once in a while a congregation will weather this stormy period and come out on the other side more passionate for Jesus and reflective of God's character. More often, the new leader gets crucified for the sake of the tradition.

Jesus helps us to understand all this with his words about garments and patches and wine and wineskins. In both metaphors there is something old being matched inappropriately with something new, and damage ensues. The new patch tears away from the old garment. The new wine in its fermenting bursts the old, brittle wineskins. The most obvious way to apply this in context is to say that Jesus is bringing a new wine into the calcified tradition of the Jewish people, and the interaction of the two is going to do violence.

What are the "new wineskins" Jesus uses to package his new wine?

- He calls people as his followers who the tradition deemed unacceptable. Jesus called tax collectors, fishermen, the demon-possessed, the poor, the outcast. He heals, loves, equips, and sends them.

- Jesus rejects the traditional interpretations of laws about Sabbath, food, who a good Jewish person should associate with, and more.
- He demands that the claims of God on a person or a community supersede the claims of the tradition.
- He refuses to be categorized when it comes to attitudes about Rome or Herod or the priesthood or the temple. He seems willing to work with all of these powers if they are in appropriate subjection to the kingship of God; he speaks judgment and destruction on each if they refuse to submit to God's kingship.
- Jesus enacts and models a new kind of relationship with God. It is a relationship not based on law but on love. His followers continue to proclaim this.
- After Jesus' death and resurrection, his followers practice some new wineskins: Sunday worship, the Lord's Supper, baptism, acceptance of believing Gentiles, lack of loyalty to the temple or to Jerusalem, willingness to coexist but not compromise with Rome. They abandon many of the traditional markers, the old wineskins. They let go of the requirements of Sabbath observance, kosher food laws, and circumcision.
- It is worth noting that expanded roles of women (and a deep, rich sense of the value of women) is an integral part of Jesus' ministry and of his church moving forward. Those today who grasp at a few verses that seem to limit the role of women in the church fail to recognize what an amazing transition

was happening from a totally patriarchal culture toward one where women gained full acceptance in Jesus' movement. In the face of the contemporary cultural realities, statements like Paul's words that there is "neither male nor female" are indicators of the radical new wine Jesus was bringing to God's good creation of male and female. Now, in the kingdom, this identity is to be lived out in partnership. Even Paul's statement that a woman should learn at home (this was radically permissive in world where the idea of women learning at all was laughable to most people!) is radically permissive for its time. Jesus' own choice of Mary Magdalene to be the first witness of the resurrection (and messenger to the male disciples!) is a mind-blowing new wineskin.

And of course there is so much more. This, in the end, is what gets Jesus crucified. He is pouring new wine into new wineskins, and the keepers of the old refuse to allow it. Jesus rightly points out that "no one after drinking old wine desires new, for he says, 'the old is good.'" Jesus isn't talking about a finely aged bottle of wine; rather he is saying that those who are entrenched in religious or social structures that protect their comfort and power will refuse to be unseated, even in the face of the Son of God.

Questions to think about:
1. What is it like to be in a very traditional church?
2. What might the tax collectors and sinners have felt like when Jesus chose them as leaders?

3. How does Jesus' ministry empower women, in the gospels and today?
4. How can we judge if we are following Jesus' new wine versus supporting our own old wineskins?

Luke 6:1-11

Through these next few chapters of Luke's narrative it is important to remember Jesus' words about wine and wineskins. That idea, that Jesus is bringing a new wine that will not fit with the old wineskins, will be lived out in the specific arenas of Sabbath and discipleship and preaching and beyond. As we work through the following verses we'll see how each develops Jesus' claims about himself, his wine, and his wineskins.

The Sabbath functioned as one of three key markers that kept the Jews separate from the surrounding cultures. Those three were the Sabbath, circumcision, and kosher food laws. These three clearly communicated who was "in" and who was "out." Each created a tangible boundary, ensuring that the Jews recognized their distinctive identity and they didn't become "polluted" by contact with Gentiles. Without a doubt those three markers were enshrined in the Torah and had in some sense been commanded by God; but in the first century, they had become the tail that wagged the dog of Judaism. How often is it so, that something God creates for good gets broken, twisted, and then the keeping of this "law" becomes a terrible burden that impedes God's mission and God's will? Too often, I'm afraid. We have to be on our guard anytime we hear otherwise godly people taking a secondary (though good) thing and pronouncing absolutes around it. There is very little a Jesus-follower can say "never" or "always" about aside from the character of God. Even the Ten Commandments are apt to become a godless moral code instead of a life-giving covenant if we make them the touchstone of our own morality rather than arrows pointing toward a life-giving relationship with God.

So it was with the Sabbath. The rabbis of Jesus' time had lengthy debates about how they could avoid breaking the Sabbath. You can only travel so many steps from your home on the Sabbath, one said. A student asked, how do you define "home"? After some thought, the rabbi replied that home is where you leave your shoes at night. So if an observant Jew wanted to travel slightly farther on the Sabbath than the oral law allowed, he would go halfway the day before and leave his shoes along the way, return home barefoot, and he could, in good conscience, travel where he needed on the Sabbath, recovering his shoes along the way.

Such examples might seem silly to us, but the Judaism of Jesus' day was full of such debates, laws, policies and micromanagement because the Jews were deeply concerned not to break God's law. It is in this context that Jesus' disciples, walking through a grain field, roll the ripe heads of grain between their hands and enjoy the crunch of God-given abundance, and thus "break" the Sabbath. Jesus points to the scriptures, and recounts how David (whom the Bible calls a "man after God's own heart") completely broke the law by eating the bread of the

Presence in the tabernacle, and fed it to his men. Similarly, Jesus chooses to heal a man whose right hand is withered. Healing, like harvesting, was considered work, and thus forbidden on the Sabbath. Jesus chooses here and elsewhere to give life on the Sabbath. He radically reinterprets the Sabbath laws and proclaims himself "lord of the Sabbath." His new wine threatens to burst the old wineskins of brittle tradition.

What Jesus is pointing to has a couple sharp points. First, the separatism inherent in the Jewish practices of Sabbath directly contradict the Jews' God-given role as a kingdom of priests inviting all the nations to come and know God and worship him. (See Exodus 19 among other passages.) What was designed to be a life-giving discipline of rest has become a heavy burden of abusive and abused laws. Second, Jesus' own authority stands over the Jews' practices of micromanagement around the Sabbath. This is a question not of law but of character. Obviously there are laws, God-given laws, about keeping the Sabbath, remembering the Sabbath to keep it holy, the necessity of rest, etc. Those are given by a loving God for the good of his people. But the rabbis had taken a life-driving principle and made it into a burdensome set of absolutes. You Must Never. You Must Always. The loving character of God in Jesus is incensed by these life-stealing absolutes.

In John's gospel (John 10:10) Jesus will sum his role up this way, and it's a deeper statement than we can realize: "I came that they might have life, and have it abundantly." His love for his people will break any wineskin that threatens the life he brings. Where we have taken his good guidelines and made them iron-fisted ethical absolutes, he will break us in order to set us free. He frees us not to become lawbreakers, but to live in relationship with his heart that gave us good guidelines in the first place.

We need to grow to what the Bible calls maturity. This is something like a young adult who finds to their delight that they really are allowed to use the good dishes, handle the sharp knives, enjoy a glass of wine. They can do these things not in hiding, behind their parents' backs, but in the company of their parents who love them and who raised them with appropriate rules designed to help them grow into responsible adulthood.

I have been marveling the last few weeks at the amount of freedom that the whitetail does give their fawns. As I write this, I have been watching a pair of spotted fawns graze past my window and through my yard. Eventually, their mother grazed through the meadow a hundred yards away, apparently unconcerned for them. She glances up from a distance, then goes back to her grazing.

There's a wisdom in this gracious freedom: if she is the helicopter parent, hovering and controlling, her children will never grow capable and responsible on their own. She must allow them into the risky world because she's a good mother and she loves them. I have been so delighted lately to talk with my own 20-something daughters and see that kind of responsible growth into early adulthood. It's exciting! God works much the same with us. He loves us enough to give us incredible freedom, and he honors our choices, whether to shackle ourselves with niggling laws or to step out in freedom and take risks, even with the possibility of failing. He's a good Father.

Questions to think about:
1. How well did your parents do with giving you appropriate rules?
2. How does a system based on legalistic rules keep people from growing to maturity?
3. What might "abundant life" look like for you?
4. What rules and regulations might you need to set aside to experience God's freedom and love?

Luke 6:12-19

We would do well to study the intentionality of Jesus, especially as he relates to different groups of people. This is a subtle but important wineskin. A few things to note:

First, Jesus is intentional about bathing his decision in prayer. He retreats from the crowds, goes into that desolate place again (here, "the mountain") and spends the entire night in prayer. The practice of extended prayer both acknowledges our dependence and invites God's intervention. It sets up a pliability in us that God honors by providing direction. Of course, it's better to approach prayer with a heart of "God, what do you want?" rather than "God, here's what I want." But God will meet you where you are and mold you from there. At the same time, it's worth sharing the desires of your heart with God, because often he delights to give you those things as a way of showing his love for you. It is the ongoing conversation with him that is important.

Second, Jesus is intentional about choosing a limited number of disciples who will be his closest followers. Without a doubt, hundreds of others followed him from time to time. In the first chapter of Acts, we learn that there were others outside the Twelve who had been with Jesus throughout his ministry. This key decision is about Jesus narrowing his relational focus. In reality, each of us has a limited amount of relational energy to expend, and that was true of Jesus in his incarnation as well.

More often than not we drift through life accepting whatever relationships happen to be our reality at this moment. We miss out on so much in this way. Jesus demonstrates that the prayerful choosing of relationships is a God-honoring thing. He was probably criticized for this. It might have seemed to some that he was playing favorites, that his movement was exclusive and not "fair." But Jesus intentionally chose the Twelve. Within the Twelve he chose Peter, James, and John to be his inner circle. Any follower of Jesus would do well to be intentional about where they invest their relational energy. Too often the mediocre, unexamined connections in our lives keep us stuck and in limbo. We need to follow those who lead us toward Christ, be sharpened by partnerships with excellence, and invest in those who can grow and develop the most from our example and efforts. Over and over throughout his ministry we see Jesus being intentional about these decisions.

Third, Jesus intentionally lays out relationships with people at various levels of connection to himself. He doesn't shut out the crowds, but he limits his time with them. He ministers to those in need of healing, but he doesn't recruit from that pool for leadership in his movement. (Mary Magdalene and the Gerasene demoniac might be two exceptions to this.) Jesus does intentionally invest time in the hurting, the curious, the hungry. But his most focused energy, the relationships at the core of his life, overwhelmingly involve those he has intentionally chosen.

The content of what Jesus shares with those disciples is yet another way Jesus creates new wine packaged in new wineskins. That's where Luke leads us next.

Questions to think about:
1. What is it like to be someone's favorite? What is it like to be outside the "favorite" group?
2. What is the difference between praying "God, what do you want?" vs. "God, here's what I want"?
3. When have you bathed a decision in prayer? Was your experience in that decision making process different from just making a decision on your own?
4. Are you intentional about the relationships you invest in? Why / why not?

Luke 6:20-36

Luke tells a slightly different story of the Sermon on the Mount than Matthew's better-known version. This should not surprise or disturb us. Christians and skeptics are sometimes put off balance by discrepancies between the different gospel accounts. An Enlightenment based standard of exactitude combined with a skepticism that is constantly on the lookout for reasons not to believe creates this kind of problem for us.

In reality, there are good reasons why these accounts might differ. For one, Luke tells us that he used other source material, and he was no doubt familiar with Matthew's construction of the "Sermon on the Mount" (Matthew 5-7). But Matthew was writing for a largely Jewish audience, and Luke is writing as a Gentile for a Gentile audience, specifically a Roman official. That will shape the narrative.

Another factor that is usually overlooked is that Jesus would likely have told the same stories and preached the same messages over and over again. And it's entirely possible that Matthew's narrative reflects one of these occasions when Jesus was preaching on a hillside, and Luke has interviewed other sources who remember a time when Jesus preached a very similar message but on a "level place" (Luke 6:17). There is no necessary discrepancy. A third factor, of course, has to do with the nature of human memory. Different people experiencing a momentous event (a car accident, for example) will vary significantly in their recounting of the details, even though the main facts are the same. (This is why the varying accounts of the resurrection in the four gospels, for example, reinforce rather than contradict one another.) In short, we should not be disturbed by the variance between Matthew's and Luke's accounts of Jesus' teaching.

It is the content of the teaching that is truly remarkable. Here again, we see Jesus providing new wine that must be packaged in new wineskins. Jesus takes our preconceived notions of God and turns them on their heads. Where we imagine God as a righteous, perhaps vindictive, judge, Jesus says his Father is in fact merciful, pouring out blessing on the ungrateful and the evil. (BTW this is the same message, by implication, that alienated his townsfolk in Nazareth in Luke 4.)

Jesus lifts up those the world is ready to discard. He castigates those the world envies. He expands the target of love immeasurably, insisting that love should include enemies. Reflect the nature of God, Jesus says, and stop creating God in your own image.

How can we have an accurate picture of who this enemy-loving God is? This points us to the greatest mistake that is made with Jesus' teaching: You can't have Jesus' teaching without him being at the center of it. Jesus is the king of the kingdom he is proclaiming. You can't have just comforting platitudes based on Jesus' message. Instead, this is a radical recasting of human existence under the uncompromising lordship of Jesus himself. In essence, Jesus says: I am coming as king. Here is what my kingdom is like. It is a kingdom of love for all, including enemies, because of who I am.

At that point, as C.S. Lewis and others have pointed out, it is not workable to say Jesus is simply a great teacher. He is Lord, and these are the principles by which one lives in his kingdom. Or, failing that, he is either lying intentionally, or he is a self-absorbed lunatic who was rightly killed as a public menace. While he is in fact a great teacher, the heart of his teaching is his own identity.

Christians have struggled mightily with these teachings over the centuries. Some have said this is an idealized system that is not attainable by human effort. Others have said that only a few elite Christians—martyrs, or monks, or saints—will be able to reach these lofty goals. Perhaps the reason these statements ("Blessed are you who are poor, for yours is the kingdom of God") seem so far beyond us is because they reflect the values of God himself.

The best explication of these teachings that I know is in Dietrich Bonhoeffer's *The Cost of Discipleship.* Bonhoeffer lays out how these kingdom principles are serious guidelines that set a standard not only for the individual believer, but also for the Jesus-focused community. They are kingdom principles. Our churches will reflect them if we are kingdom communities.

Questions to think about:
1. Have you heard people say they believe Jesus was just a great teacher? What do you think?
2. How do you see Jesus revealing the heart of God in these teachings?
3. What do you think of Lewis' comment that Jesus is either liar, lunatic or Lord?
4. What is it like to live as part of a community that is striving toward living out Jesus' teachings?

Luke 6:37-42

We assume that God shares our concerns about perfectionism and moral rectitude. In our pride we think that our ethical standards, whether we apply them mercilessly to ourselves or to others, reflect God's own heart. In nothing are we farther from the example of Jesus.

I had a conversation a few months ago with a man who told me that Jesus' words about the log in your own eye and the speck in your brother's eye meant that first, yes, we should deal with our own sin. But then we are expected, even commanded, to judge our brother and point out his sin. I was flabbergasted. How could a reasonable person read these verses and come to the conclusion that we are commanded to stand in judgment over others? The answer, of course, is that none of us are reasonable people. We come with our own preconceptions and assumptions shaping our reading of the text. How can we get through all that interference to hear Jesus for what he is really saying?

This requires the careful work of God's Spirit over time, to expose and strip away the colored glasses that so tint our perceptions. Our bedrock assumptions are hardest of all to see. So often our bedrock assumption is that we do bad things and that God is angry because we do bad things. This childish understanding of morality has never been exposed to the light, and so we never come to realize the good news of Jesus.

Understand, God does not take sin lightly. Our sin stands as a barrier between us and God, and he will never make light of that. The good news is that we have been completely mistaken about God's attitude toward *us*. Jesus repeatedly speaks and models that God is mercy and kindness and love, even toward sinners. The people whose sin Jesus railed against were those who a) claimed to speak for God, and b) ruthlessly condemned those who did not meet their standard of moral behavior.

Again, God is not cavalier about sin. The problem with sinful behavior is that it puts up a barrier to a loving relationship with God. But don't miss this: The problem with an ungodly focus on sin is that it puts up a barrier to a loving relationship with God.

I'm always amazed what we hear Jesus saying in texts like this. When Jesus says, "A disciple is not above his teacher but everyone when he is fully trained will be like his teacher," what picture comes to your mind? More often than not we will immediately focus on Jesus' moral perfection, on his sinlessness, on his absolutely seamless relationship with his Father, etc. But if God has given you the severe gift of brokenness, it is possible to hear these words in a completely different way, here and throughout the gospels. In the margin of my Bible next to this verse is a note I wrote in one of the lowest periods of my life: It starts with the date I wrote it, and then these words: "Despised, rejected, acquainted w/ grief, one from whom men hide their faces, numbered with sinners, friend of tax collectors and prostitutes." This was Jesus' earthly reputation. That is exactly how I felt at that low point in my life. What does it mean to be fully trained to be like this teacher, like Jesus?

Perhaps Jesus' words about the log and the speck are designed to teach us humility. Instead of striving for sinlessness in terms of ethical perfection, perhaps we need to learn to come to God fully aware of our own wretchedness but also fully aware of his open-armed love and mercy. Maybe we need to learn to extend that same open-armed love and mercy to those around us without first speaking condemnation over their sin. That's the way Jesus modeled the character of God. That's the measure (v. 38) he calls us to use.

Questions to think about:
1. What does it feel like to have something stuck in your eye? What about when it's removed?
2. What does it take to show mercy to a person who deserves judgment?
3. Has God ever given you the "severe gift of brokenness"? What was that like?
4. What does it mean, in this context, to be like Jesus?

Luke 6:43-49

Here Jesus makes explicit the new wine and the new wineskin of his kingdom: "Why do you call me 'Lord, Lord,' and not do what I tell you?" This kingdom revolves around its king and his loving rule. The power of this kingdom lies not in a set of principles but in a relationship with the king, Jesus. Through him we relate to the Father, the God he reveals to us. This is the heart of Christianity; this is the heart of the abundant life Jesus comes to give.

This is the key to Jesus' word that "out of the abundance of the heart the mouth speaks." He wants to be the treasure at the heart of our lives, and we will never experience the abundance of life unless we value him above all else. We may love to quote the psalm about God giving us the desires of our hearts, but we need to remember the previous line: "Delight yourself in the Lord, and he will give you the desire of your heart."

We have other treasures, of course: activities, possessions, relationships that are tremendously valuable to us. But these treasures must be subordinate in our affections. Jesus demands the freedom to marshal and order these other treasures. He brings them to the fore and drives them out of the limelight in his own timing. In his wisdom, there are seasons for these other treasures. Both our debilitating anxieties and our driving to grasp for control reveal that we don't trust Jesus fully with the ordering of our treasures.

Part of learning kingdom wisdom is learning that timing is critical for these other treasures to be life-giving rather than life-taking. This is one dimension of Jesus' words about fig trees and thornbushes. A good gift grasped in the wrong timing can become a curse. Left in the hands of Jesus, it becomes a blessing. In the moment when he opens doors and gives gracious freedom, we take hold with humility, trust, and thanksgiving. Then this powerful gift serves the abundance for which Jesus created it. Timing is important, and only by keeping Jesus as our supreme treasure can we receive all things else for our good.

This is a hard discipline to learn. The New Testament is full of this kind of hard wisdom. Paul writes hard words in Romans 5 about suffering producing endurance producing character producing hope. The author of Hebrews writes hard words in Hebrews 12 about enduring discipline as beloved children, though it doesn't seem pleasant at the time. We may well pine for a longed-for gift (a career advancement, a healing, a relationship, an adventure) and the desire may drive us a long way down the road toward despair. It is in this painful longing that Jesus does much of his best work to shape and form us. The waiting tempers us, preparing a strong foundation of faith for the day when the floods come.

Along the way, there will be smaller tempests. We will experience tremendous trials and it will feel like the foundations of our lives are crumbling. Jesus is using these trials. He is preparing us, not punishing us. He uses them at times to drive us to our knees so that we come to a place of trusting him at a deeper level. Other times he is pointing out elements of our lives that need to be cut off because they have become deadly. There is a time to endure, and a time to set a firm boundary and say "Enough!" Discerning the difference is only possible if Jesus is our ultimate treasure, the one we not only call "Lord" but also obey.

1. What might it mean to "delight yourself in the Lord"?
2. Is it hard or easy for you to trust God when it comes to your own desires and his timing? Why?
3. How does the experience of difficulty build us toward character and maturity?
4. Is Jesus your ultimate treasure? What evidence supports your answer?

Luke 7:1-17

Remember that Jesus is living out the new wine in new wineskins throughout these chapters. His kingdom and his kingship stand in stark contrast to the ironclad rules of human existence as they have been known in the past.

There are a couple absolutes of this world that Jesus contradicts in these verses. The first rule is, "Our tribe above all others." The second is, "Death has the final say."

The Roman centurion is a perfect example of one who not only calls Jesus "Lord" (see the last verses of chapter 6) but also puts a life-changing trust in him. Through the rigid structures and ironclad obedience of the Roman army, God has given himself a witness in this man's life. The centurion uses his military experience and authority to put himself under Jesus' authority. His submission is a remarkable testimony both to Jesus and the Jews. Interestingly, the Jews surrounding Jesus make a claim that the centurion deserves Jesus' attention because of his good works, but the centurion himself makes no such claim. Instead he defers to Jesus' power and mercy, never trying to argue for his own way.

The dead man, of course, is beyond any appeal at all. Death is just the final, despairing end of all things. Except that Jesus turns even this certainty on its head. Instead of the hopelessness of a mother stumbling along in her son's funeral procession, Jesus creates wonder, awe, and new life.

Both of these incidents point to the supreme kingly authority of Jesus himself. These actions are parables-in-action. In the first, the hated outsider, the Roman oppressor, submits to God's grace. He is a representative of "all the nations" who will be blessed through Abraham's descendants (see Genesis 12). The raising of the widow's son at Nain (a minor village in southeastern Galilee, about five miles from Nazareth) flies in the face of the grief and hopelessness death always brings. The Old Testament is full of many statements about the finality of death, and there are just a few remarkable hope-filled spots where it hints that God might someday defeat even death. Jesus takes what has only been hinted and lives it out in full glory.

We often miss an element in this story–the mother herself. Luke is careful to tell us that the man is the only son of his mother, and that she is a widow. Luke also says specifically that Jesus had compassion *on her*. It is hard for us to understand the economic terror that faced this woman. As a widow deprived of her only son, she now had no means of support, no rights, no status. She would be consigned to begging at best. When Jesus raises the young man, we are told Jesus gives him specifically to his mother. Jesus not only resuscitates the young man's dead body, but he gives the woman back her life as well. Luke is very good at showing us how Jesus pays attention to women. He treats them as fully human, bearers of the image of God, partners in his ministry and more. Again, it is difficult for us to envision how far outside the norms this was in Jesus' day. He stands as king in a kingdom that contradicts the ironclad rules of our existence.

The people of his own day had trouble understanding who Jesus was and what he had come to accomplish. That's what we'll see next time as even John the Baptist starts to question Jesus' work.

Questions to think about:
1. What is most surprising about the Roman centurion's actions? Jesus' actions?
2. What surprising ways have you seen God leave himself a witness in people's lives?
3. Do you suppose it was stressful for the widow to turn from grief to joy so quickly? Why / why not?
4. Imagine the gossip about these two incidents around Galilee in the next few days. What might that have been like?

Luke 7:18-23

Have you ever been embroiled in a scandal? Scandals have little to do with fact; usually they erupt because people's expectations don't match with actual events OR with the inflated report of events. In our day of fake news, scandals are commonplace. Much of what passes for news is in fact just the latest scandal. We gravitate toward the manufactured outrage of expectation and disappointment.

Messengers come to Jesus from John the Baptist. Jesus sends them back to report what they have seen and heard: People are being healed. That widow in Nain received her dead son back alive. Demons are being overthrown. Good news of God's kingly rule is being preached to the disenfranchised. Jesus ends the message with a curious statement: "Blessed is the one who is not offended by me." The Greek word for offended here is the word from which we get our English word "scandalized." Jesus knows he doesn't match people's expectations. His identity and ministry doesn't match people's expectations for a Messiah. That's why many people—especially the keepers of the old wineskins—will be scandalized by him.

Even John the Baptist who announced Jesus to the people in the beginning is struggling. It is significant that the same question is repeated verbatim at the beginning of this section: "Are you the one who is to come, or should we look for another?" The people had been waiting a long time, and anticipation ran high. John had been convinced that Jesus was the Messiah. God himself had spoken to John and revealed this. But while Jesus was obviously a prophet and a healer with a potent message of God's kingship, he wasn't doing all those expected Messiah things. He wasn't restoring the glory of the nation, throwing off the Roman oppressors, purifying the temple.

It's easy to sympathize with John. He might well be in Herod's prison already at this time. At any rate he is seeing the movement he began shifting its momentum over to the wandering healer, Jesus. Has John run his race in vain? Did he in fact hear God incorrectly? Was the vision just his own imagining? Have you ever been in this position? You believe that God has revealed himself to you in some specific way and then you wait. You wait for the vision to be accomplished. Will it be fulfilled? You may have felt that same pit-of-the-stomach fear John's question betrays. Come on, Jesus, get on about the business of being Messiah! Make it happen! Do it now!

Jesus' answer to John is instructive. Basically Jesus challenges John in return: Do you have eyes to see? Do you have ears to hear? Look what's going on around you. Jesus' identity as Messiah is far greater than a warrior at the head of an army or a zealot demanding ethical conduct of the priesthood. In effect Jesus says, "I may not be good news for the leaders of political movements who are concerned about their own legacy, but I am good news for the blind, the lame, the poor, the lepers. Are you willing to see your own need?" Next to Jesus' list in the margin of my Bible I've written a date and the brief note, "A season of being all these needy things." It is hard to live in that desperately needy place. It's hard to wait in pain. But for those who know their need, Jesus is good news. He fulfills the passage from Isaiah 61 he quoted at the synagogue in Nazareth (Luke 4). Sadly, like the people of Nazareth, John the Baptist has a different set of expectations.

The critical point for us is to see our own expectations clearly and bring them into line with Jesus. Yes, there is a chance we have mistaken the initial vision God gave. So we may be disappointed when Jesus doesn't fulfill it the way we would like. It is far more likely, however, if we have done our homework and prayerfully tested what we thought God was up to, that the vision God has given simply requires more time than we realized. What seems simple to us may be only one facet of a greater adventure into which God is leading us. It may take more time to coordinate all those facets, to reveal all the different dimensions of wonder God is preparing for us. At the same time we ourselves are growing into the vision. When it first appeared, no matter what we thought at the time, we were probably not ready to receive it.

It's worth noting, too, that Jesus doesn't condemn John for his question. He will go on at some length to defend John in the coming verses.

Questions to think about:
1. Have you ever had to wait patiently for something? What was it like?
2. Imagine that John the Baptist is in prison when he sends the messengers. What is at stake for him?

3. How can you seek to understand God's agenda more fully? What does that take?
4. What do you feel when you consider that you might not be ready to receive all God wants to give you?

Luke 7:24-35

John the Baptist created a massive quake in Jewish circles in the first century. Today we'd describe his movement as something between a Billy Graham revival and a Lady Gaga concert. He had both the fascination of a strangely dressed rock star and the awe of a judgmental preacher. Biblical and secular historians are consistent in describing massive crowds headed out of the cities into the desert when John started preaching and baptizing. Jesus echoes these descriptions by asking three times, "What did you go out in the desert to see?" The assumption is that all the people listening, or at least the vast majority, had actually gone to see John and to be baptized by him. No one in those days would have denied that there was something big happening in John's ministry. The question was, what authority was behind John the Baptist? Was his movement from God, or just a strange human spectacle?

Jesus goes on at length here to challenge people's thinking about John, and to lay out how he himself sees John's ministry. Luke tells us that there is a significant divide between the common people who had been baptized by John and those (religious authorities) who refused his baptism and thus "rejected the purpose of God for themselves." Shortly before his crucifixion, Jesus turned this question succinctly on his detractors: The baptism of John, was it from heaven or from man? (See Luke 20:4 and parallels in Matthew and Mark.) The rulers at that time answer Jesus, "We don't know" because they recognize their culpability in rejecting John's baptism. They also fear the people. In their defensive pride, they dodge the question poorly.

Jesus makes clear that God was behind John's revival. Not only that, but John was the specific individual sent to prepare the way for Jesus. He was sent to stir up people's spiritual sensitivities so they were ready for the Messiah. The confusing phraseology of verse 28 is designed to point out that as a divinely chosen agent, John wields great power in purely human terms. But anyone who submits to God's rule and serves at the pleasure of the King of Kings is far more powerful.

This passage is a great example of the Bible's view of judgment. We sometimes see Jesus portrayed as a judge. He sits on a throne and passes sentence. Good people who receive his favor go to one side and evil people who receive his condemnation go to the other. In fact, judgment, and Jesus' role as judge, are much simpler and less dramatic. The Jewish religious leaders condemned themselves because when God showed up, in their arrogance they rejected John and refused his baptism. That's the judgment. They already chose sides. We see people judging themselves throughout Jesus' ministry by their response to him. He is the "judge" because he gives people an opportunity to choose. Jesus represents God and his kingdom. He stands for God and not for any human faction. So when we face him we are forced to submit or rebel.

This pattern repeats itself over and over even today. When God shows up, we are judged based on a) whether we have eyes to see him and his activity, and b) how we respond. So in the 1970's and 80's, a massive Christian charismatic renewal swept the world. Churches all over the world responded very differently to this renewal. In East Africa, the Tanzanian Lutheran Church embraced this charismatic dimension while still trying to be theologically responsible about it. Across the border to the north, the Kenyan Lutherans rejected it, claiming that any kind of charismatic activity was inappropriate for Lutheran Christians. The Tanzanian Lutheran churches grew and flourished, multiplying hundreds of times over. The Kenyan Lutheran church to this day is a very small, very rigid affair. Kenya has experienced massive religious revivals, but the Lutheran church there has remained largely outside this God-given growth.

Whenever God shows up, people have the opportunity to respond. Some will get on board and say, "I see God doing a great thing here." No surprise, others will reject Spirit-driven change and along with it, reject the leaders God provides. Accusations fly. Leaders are broken and lambasted. Churches divide. In many cases, people's rejection of a particular leadership agenda for positive change means they are rejecting a God-given opportunity for growth and renewal. The public conversation becomes about personalities and reputations.

We should not be surprised by these sad situations. Jesus himself went to the cross in a very similar chain of events. Given that, how should sinful, imperfect human leaders expect anything less? The miracle in all this is that God gets his own way, no matter how hard he has to work to make it happen. So John ends up imprisoned and executed by Herod, but the revival he initiates paves the way for Jesus' ministry. Jesus goes to the cross, and his crucifixion becomes the ultimate opportunity for us to judge ourselves. We can submit to him and receive the embrace of his nail-scarred hands, or stand aside and do things our own way. We can reject God's purpose for us. Jesus' resurrection becomes the ultimate example of God enacting his kingdom in spite of our rejection. Our judging God—and that is really what it comes down to—cannot prevent him from being king.

In the end, John is an amazing example of what it means to surrender our own human power and authority. In John's gospel, John the Baptist says of Jesus, "He must increase, but I must decrease." John, the ultimate revival preacher, submits his agenda and his authority to Jesus. That is not a bad way to start each day. Simply say, "Jesus, I want your way today. More of you, and less of me in my life."

Questions to think about:
1. How is "judgment" described in this section? Is this different than the way you've usually viewed it?
2. Why do you suppose people had such radically different responses to John, or to Jesus?

3. How can we discern whether a movement is from God or just of human origin?
4. What might it mean today for you to pray, "Lord, I want you to increase and me to decrease"?

Luke 7:36-50

Certain factions of Christians have made a cornerstone of their faith that the holiness of God cannot exist in the presence of sin. This principle then drives the need for the cross and Jesus' vicarious atonement for us. Unfortunately for them, the Bible doesn't seem to share their view of how God's holiness functions. God goes looking for Adam and Eve after they sin. God creates a Tent of Meeting for the Israelites so they can meet with him. God certainly doesn't take sin lightly. God is holy, and sin rightly invites God's wrath and judgment. Yet in the Bible God is constantly seeking out sinners and welcoming them, specifically with the goal of making them holy with his own holiness. This story of Jesus welcoming the sinful woman in the home of Simon the Pharisee is Exhibit A.

Simon seems to have this same "God can't be in the presence of sin" understanding of the holiness of God. If Jesus was a prophet, Simon thinks, he'd toss this woman out. In other words if Jesus had access to the perspective of God's holiness, he would never tolerate this woman's presence, let alone touch. She's a sinner. Jesus, on the other hand, seems to delight in keeping company with sinful humans. (Let's be clear: Jesus loves these people.

He does not love their sin.) This mystifies us. How could this be? His parable provides a beginning. It is forgiveness, not sinlessness, that opens the door to fellowship with Jesus. The woman's desire to be with Jesus is driven by the sense she has that she is welcomed by Jesus. As far as we read, she pays zero attention to Simon the Pharisee, though he is a powerful, upstanding member of the community. She is not currying favor or looking to advance her own cause. She is a grateful heart desiring the fellowship into which being forgiven has ushered her.

We must constantly be on guard against making Jesus and his message about sin management. Simon seems to be operating from the assumption that the less sin you commit the better. Most of us would agree with that. And yes, it is better to do right than to do wrong, of course. But Jesus seems to have a slightly different frame of reference. Jesus says she loves much, and he seems to value that immensely. If loving much is the goal, then being forgiven much seems to be the pathway toward that goal.

Be careful here. This hairline we are trying to walk is precisely why Paul, at the beginning of Romans 6, has to put out a disclaimer: "Shall we continue in sin so that God's grace may abound? By no means!" The issue is not that we should make sure we are sinful enough. Rather, the issue is that we should make sure we recognize the depth of our own sinfulness. The trouble with Simon is that he doesn't know his own sinfulness. Therefore he doesn't recognize the magnitude of his own forgiveness. And so he doesn't throw himself at Jesus' feet. Our churches are full of Simons who engage in tepid, self-righteous worship because they don't really believe they need much forgiveness. They look down their noses at those who do. They are already pretty good people. Just ask them.

There's another interesting facet to this story. Given Luke's penchant for detail and accuracy, well attested by everyone who has ever studied Luke & Acts in depth, it's hard to reconcile this version of the story with those in Matthew, Mark, & John. In those three gospels, the woman is Mary of Bethany who anoints Jesus out of gratitude for his raising her brother Lazarus. She does so immediately before Jesus' betrayal and arrest. Luke places the story much earlier in Jesus' ministry, and the woman is a prostitute. The entire incident functions differently in Luke's gospel. While it's not necessary or helpful to try to reconcile the gospels at every turn—different witnesses to the same events often tell slightly different versions—this story has stuck in my craw over the years. I've come to the belief that a few interesting possibilities are in fact likely:

- I believe Simon the Pharisee, referred to elsewhere as Simon the Leper, was the father of Mary, Martha, and Lazarus and they all lived in Bethany, just east of Jerusalem.
- I believe that Simon came to be a follower of Jesus and opened his home to Jesus. Lazarus and his sisters seem to have continued this practice.
- I believe that Simon died sometime during the course of Jesus' ministry, leaving Lazarus in charge of his household.

- Luke's version of this story of the sinful woman takes place early in Jesus' ministry when Simon and Jesus are first getting acquainted.
- Matthew, Mark, and John tell about another incident entirely. When Mary, overcome with gratitude, is looking for a way to express her devotion to Jesus, she intentionally imitates what she saw this woman do months or even years earlier.

Other explanations are possible, but there are numerous elements in the biblical story that make sense this way. In the end, it doesn't matter much. This incident in Luke's gospel gives us enough to chew on by itself.

Questions to think about:
1. How do you think the other people seated at the table might have felt about the woman's actions?
2. How might this woman have felt when Jesus defended her actions?
3. What is the difference between sinlessness and being forgiven? Who is the focus of each?
4. Why do you suppose Jesus contrasts loving much and loving little? What is he getting at?

Luke 8:1-21

So often we take Jesus' parables, his miracles, the other narratives like distinct little nuggets, each to be consumed in isolation. Nothing could be further from the truth. Luke (and the other New Testament writers) are carefully crafting their work to a) be faithful witnesses to the actual events of Jesus' ministry, his death and resurrection. They also b) use their artistic abilities as writers to make the narrative into more than a collection of stories like pearls on a string. So it is in this chapter: The handful of verses that open chapter eight highlight some women who are incredibly important to the story. Each deserves to be researched in her own right, but together they stand with the lepers being healed, the demoniacs being delivered, the blind receiving their sight. In a society where women had roughly the same rights as cattle (and sometimes less), Jesus makes them a key part of his entourage. They are individuals, people, precious children of God. This is part of the new wineskin into which Jesus pours the wine of his message about the kingdom of God. What's more, these women by their following faithfully demonstrate that they are good soil—and what's more, they will join the men in becoming faithful sowers of the gospel seed.

That's really the point of the story Jesus tells next. Most sermons on "the parable of the soils" delve into the question, "What kind of soil am I?" But Jesus is telling this story from a very different perspective. He's positing the disciples as seed-sowers, and the parable functions as a cautionary tale: Most of the seeds you plant won't bear fruit.

Notice that bearing fruit is Jesus' concern. Jesus repeatedly tells his disciples that the goal of their discipleship is bearing fruit (see John 15, for example). Sowing the seed into good soil should produce fruit. That's the entire point of this parable and so many others Jesus tells. We make "the gospel" a narrative about how we can get to heaven. Trouble is, we can only make it fit our theological framework by doing terrible violence to Jesus' own teaching. By the New Testament's logic, a believer who is unfruitful might in fact enter heaven, but they would do so only in some kind of disgrace. This seems to be exactly Paul's argument in 1 Corinthians 3, for example. In that chapter Paul talks about building on a foundation with various materials. Poorer quality materials (wood, hay, straw) would be burned up in a fiery judgment. The builder might be saved, he says, but only through fire. Their unfruitful work is consumed in the judgment.

Jesus is not saving souls for a distant heaven. He is gathering followers to tell the world that God is king. God's kingdom is being inaugurated at last. This is the startling good news. This is the message the disciples are sent to scatter on all kinds of soil. This is the message that shines like a lamp on a stand, that redefines family such that Jesus says even his own mother and brothers are redefined by the king and his kingdom. God's rule, God's kingship, changes everything.

So Jesus seems to say to us, be careful how you hear. Don't listen within the stale categories of that old time religion you've always found boring. Recognize that I am doing something new, and I'm calling you to be a part of it. Let that seed sprout and put down deep roots into your soul, into your heart. Let it bear fruit. Come, follow me.

1. How do Luke's spare comments about the women who follow Jesus introduce the parable of the soils?
2. In what ways does picturing yourself as the sower change the way you read this parable?
3. How might focusing on "bearing fruit" create a different faith than focus on "going to heaven"?
4. Do you agree that "God is king, and his kingdom is here" is Jesus' basic message? Why / why not?

Luke 8:22-39

These two stories are usually handled separately but they are a unit, both with the same theme. There are two key verses here. First, verse 25 ("Who is this, that even the wind and waves obey him?"). Second, verse 39, where Luke draws an explicit verbal conclusion that Jesus is God. That is the witness of the man who has been delivered from a legion of demons. The focus of both stories is on Jesus.

In both stories, Jesus upsets the established order. He is, in Jackson Browne's memorable words, "the rebel Jesus;" his authority overturns what we have come to expect as normal. We know that the weather is beyond our control, but Jesus stills the storm. Who is he? We know that demon possession is beyond our control, but Jesus deals with a legion of demons out of hand. Who is he? The stories return again and again to this question, implicitly and explicitly.

People today tend to evaluate Christianity based on the behavior of the church. The church certainly needs to regulate and monitor itself, and there is an enormous responsibility for the church to reflect Jesus' character. But judging Christianity based on the church is a little like judging a restaurant based on its website. (And yes, people often do just that.) The real test is Jesus himself, and he alone lies at the heart of his movement. Churches, structures, hypocrisy, liturgies, factions, boredom—none of this sticks to Jesus.

Notice that Jesus inspires fear in both segments of this story. We get entrenched in our own assumptions. As a teacher of mine once said, we prefer comfortable problems over uncomfortable solutions. The disciples go from terror in the storm to being afraid about Jesus and his identity. The people of Gerasa are consumed by terror and ask Jesus to leave their area. Even though he has just set free a man they had tried and failed to liberate, they cannot get excited about Jesus remaining among them. They are in every kind of terror—economic, spiritual, social. Their fear prevents them from welcoming the healing Jesus brings.

Perhaps the most chilling word in the whole story is in verse 37: "So". Because of their fear and their rejection of Jesus, he leaves their area. The uncomfortable biblical truth is that Jesus will honor our rejection of him. They have seen his power in undeniable fashion and rather than embrace his authority and the kingdom he announces, they send him home to his own side of the lake.

When Jesus comes to us he will not leave things the same. Jesus will not leave our established idolatries unchallenged. When we settle for "good enough," Jesus challenges us to live for him and for his kingdom. When we give in to the idolatry of our own comfort, Jesus invites us into adventure. But he will not force us to come along.

The good news is that being close to Jesus is both the safest and most exciting place to be. It may not feel safe, of course. Jesus surrounds himself with disruption of relationships and hierarchies. But the abundant life of following Jesus is far better than our cracked good-enough wineskins.

As I ponder this story, that is where my mind so often comes to rest. I think about the death-filled existence of the townspeople, the swineherds, and especially the pre-Jesus demoniac. The description of his life in Mark's gospel (Mark 5) is especially vivid. Maybe the demon-possessed man thought it was good enough to live among the tombs, to gash himself with stones, to occasionally venture into town bound with chains until the powers overcame him and he broke loose to terrorize the neighbors. It was certainly all he could expect, given his spiritual condition. But Jesus wanted so much more for him. At the end of the story, this man is miraculously free precisely because he recognizes that Jesus is the one who has freed him. The townspeople who reject Jesus are the ones left in chains.

Maybe you are feeling bound today. Social convention or established orders or death-filled existence that doesn't seem to include hope, or by economic structures that keep

you in chains… any of these may keep you bound.,
Imagine yourself a demon possessed man sitting among
the gravestones on the hilltop above the lakeshore,
watching a boat arrive on the beach below. You watch a
dozen or so men get out of the boat and come up the
hillside toward you. There is something about the figure
leading the procession. Inside your chest where there has
only been torment and death and hopelessness for so
long, something stirs like a baby kicking in the womb:
Hope.

<u>Questions to think about:</u>
1. What is the most surprising thing in this story, do
   you think?
2. What are the parallels between Jesus calming the
   storm and Jesus casting out the legion of demons?
3. In what ways are you living in some kind of chains?
   What might it look like to be set free?
4. How do you react to the statement that Jesus will
   honor our rejection of him?

Luke 8:40-56

These two stories—Jesus raising Jairus' daughter and the
healing of the woman who seeks to touch Jesus in the
crowd—are woven together in a single unit. They seem like
odd stories to weave together, and there may be several
reasons for the juxtaposition.

First, both stories confront things that are beyond human
ability to change. The woman has experienced a flow of

blood for twelve years and Luke (the physician) makes clear that no human doctor was able to heal her. Though she had exhausted all her resources on physicians, no one could help her. Her condition apparently caused her some distress physically, as she could tell immediately that she was healed. What's more, such a flow of blood would have made her perpetually ritually unclean according to the Jewish laws. This is not only a medical but also a religious, spiritual, and social problem for her.

The twelve year old girl's problem is more straightforward: she is dying. Her father, a man of standing among his neighbors, a leader within the Jewish faith, humbles himself because he has no power over his daughter's sickness. He is hopeless without Jesus. Anyone with any sense of empathy can imagine Jairus' impatience as Jesus pauses to deal with this woman. Her condition is tragic, but not immediately life-threatening. Then the dreaded messengers come: "Do not trouble the teacher any more." His beautiful daughter is dead. Hope is gone. There is no way back to joy.

Second, this entire narrative points to the authority of Jesus over situations that are beyond human control. Merely touching the fringe on Jesus' garment, even without his intention, brings healing to the woman. And death itself is redefined in his presence. (I love how Luke describes the certainty of the mourners in verse 53: "they laughed at [Jesus], knowing that she was dead.") Under Jesus' authority, death itself is redefined as a temporary thing. Jesus stands in authority over even the most ironclad of institutions. In the face of things that we cannot imagine being altered or changed, he changes them simply by his presence.

This is why it is so critically important for Jesus' followers—in that day and in this—to remain close to him. Where our human understanding runs down to despair, Jesus brings life and hope. Where we are imprisoned, whether by human institutions or physical constraints or death itself, in the presence of Jesus there is freedom.

Joy is not an illusion. Jairus must have thought that all the brightness had just gone out of his world. One can imagine all the "if-only's" running through his mind: If only I had gone to Jesus earlier. If only I had carried my daughter with me so he could have touched her. If only she hadn't gotten sick. If only Jesus hadn't stopped to deal with this woman. If only. But Jesus says, "Do not fear; only believe." Can we trust in the face of our own hopelessness? Jesus leads Jairus and his wife past the mourners, past the mockers, past those living in their certainty about the permanence of death. He leads them into the house where this girl has woken up each day for twelve years. Jesus takes her lifeless hand, as one can imagine Jairus doing each morning. Jesus speaks the words Jairus has probably spoken each day to wake her up to new life and possibility: "Child, arise." In Jesus' presence, death itself has no permanence. She opens her eyes and gets out of bed. She is free from her deadly bondage to death, restored to life and possibility, relationship and joy.

1. How do we usually deal with things that are beyond our ability to influence?
2. Why do you suppose Jesus stops to deal with the woman who touches him?
3. What emotions do you think Jairus experiences in the course of this story?
4. How are you tempted to buy into the idea that joy is an illusion? How does Jesus contradict that idea?

Luke 9:1-17

Luke 9 is a watershed chapter. We'll see in these next verses the apex of Jesus' Galilean ministry followed by a decisive turn toward the cross. It's important to realize that like a good play, the action here is rising and the conflict (which has been present all along) is intensifying.

Jesus sends the twelve out to do what he himself has been doing. This is classic discipleship. First you watch me do it, then you do it with me, then I send you out on your own to do it. By the way, churches could learn a lot from this simple model about equipping leaders for ministry.

I want to riff for a moment on one way the evangelical movement of Christianity has abused language to its detriment. Notice that Jesus sends the twelve out specifically to proclaim the kingdom of God and to heal (verse 2). That content is very specific. And in verse 6, Luke says that they went out "preaching the gospel" and healing. It is not a stretch to say that Luke equates "preaching the gospel" with "proclaiming the kingdom of God." Study this throughout the gospels and you will find the same equivalence. But too many Christians have a different definition for "the gospel." We make the gospel = *turn your heart over to Jesus so he can forgive your sins so you will go to heaven when you die.* I am convinced that much of the weakness and malaise of today's church, especially in the United States and other consumer-driven western democracies, is due to this misunderstanding of the gospel. Look what Jesus proclaimed:

- the authority and kingship of God;
- Jesus' own authority and kingship as God's chosen "Son of Man";
- the dynamics of the kingdom Jesus came to inaugurate, including healing for the lepers, recovery of sight for the blind, release for the prisoners, hope for the despairing, life for the dead.

All of this richness has been reduced down to "say a prayer so you don't spend eternity in hell." Instead of being a God-centered kingdom, we've made a self-centered insurance policy. Instead of being a set of values and lifestyles that turns this world upside down (see Acts 17) we have made it about us being eternally safe.

Don't misunderstand. Jesus' death and resurrection certainly gives us solid hope for eternity with him. He conquered death. Eternal separation from God (hell) is rightly to be feared and avoided. But my point is this: our ways of speaking and teaching about the good news of

Jesus should reflect his own words and teaching. If that is the case, we need to look hard at how Jesus spoke and taught. If we depart from Jesus' words and methods, we need to have a very good reason for doing so.

Thus endeth the riff. If you want to dig further into this topic, I strongly recommend N.T. Wright's excellent book, *Simply Good News.*

Notice the first ripple that happens because of the mission of the twelve: Herod is rocked by the impact of their message. Herod, *the king.* Herod, who has made his political bed with the Romans and has a stranglehold on the Jews and their nation. The kingdom of God shakes the rulers of this world and all their power. It turns their systems and values on their heads.

The next section (the feeding of the five thousand) echoes two major themes that would have been obvious to Jesus' original audience. First, it is a major reprise of the Exodus story. God provided bread (manna) for the Israelites in the wilderness. In a "desolate place" (verse 12) Jesus provides bread for everyone to eat, and there is more than enough. As God set the Israelites free from slavery in Egypt, Jesus' movement leads people not to freedom from physical hunger (though that is one element of it) but spiritual hunger and thirst. These themes come back again and again in the gospels. This echo of the Exodus story rings throughout this chapter and will be specifically named in the Transfiguration later in the chapter.

The second theme that would have been obvious to anyone in Jesus' original audience is that of Caesar's claim to godlike kingship. The Caesars won the people of Rome (and the empire) by providing "bread and circuses," though that is a later term. Still, Caesar's claim to be the provider of stability, including trustworthy food supplies, won the support of famine-fearing people. (Rome was able to provide stable food supplies largely because it controlled the fertile Nile delta.) Jesus' kingship flies in the face of Caesar's claims.

We tend to be amazed by the actual demonstration of divine power in multiplying food, and this story becomes a punch line at church suppers when attendance is greater than expected. "Better hope Jesus can still divide the loaves and fishes! That line is out the door!" But there is so much more going on in this narrative. Jesus is proclaiming himself the Messiah, the representative of the God of the Exodus, as well as the rightful king in the face of both Herod and Caesar.

Questions to think about:
1. Have you ever been sent into a leadership role, especially in ministry? How did that happen?
2. What is your reaction to Jeff's riff about how we define the gospel?
3. How do you respond to the idea that Jesus feeding the 5000 is both a spiritual and a political act?
4. How does the kingdom of God shake religious and political rulers in our own day?

Luke 9:18-36

There are three strong themes in this section: revelation, testimony, and challenge.

In each case—with the disciples in a private conversation, with the crowds as Jesus is teaching, and on the mountain as Jesus is transfigured—Jesus is revealed in his authority. In each case there is a testimony to his identity. Finally there is a challenge to those who experience his presence.

There is a significant danger for those of us who have been around Christianity for any length of time. We can get jaded to the amazing presence, character, and power of Jesus. We become like a man who has worked in a nuclear reactor for years and just takes all that awesome power for granted. Can we allow ourselves to confront Jesus in a new way? Can we be awed, and maybe even intimidated, by him again?

The disciples have worked and walked with Jesus. He asks them to answer the question: Who is Jesus? First he asks about others' opinions, but then about their own. They cite the answers they've heard whispered in the crowds: a prophet, Elijah, etc. Then Jesus asks them, "What do you think?" Peter speaks what the disciples have begun to suspect. He verbalizes the awesome realization that Jesus is indeed the Messiah. He is God's chosen one, not just another prophet (great as that would be) but totally unique, one of a kind. Matthew's version of this story includes

Peter naming Jesus as "the son of the living God" as well. In the first century the idea of sonship was much more about authority, of being the rightful heir, than it was about genetics. Proclaiming Jesus the Son of God meant Jesus had God's own authority. In any case, Peter voices what the disciples hardly dare think: Jesus is God's chosen agent, his authorized son, sent to enact God's plan for the Jews and for the world. Nuclear reactor indeed!

The crowd has a less intense, less clear experience that parallels what the disciples have realized close-up. They are drawn to Jesus, eager to know more about him. Have you noticed that Jesus has this affect on people? If people begin to dig into who Jesus is, he is magnetic. He draws people to himself.

Nowhere is this more true than on the mountain when Jesus is revealed in his glory, transfigured before Peter, James, and John. How could they look away from Jesus, let alone the fact that he is standing and talking with Moses and Elijah, the greatest heroes of their faith! As the conversation is winding down, Peter begins to babble, eager to create something a bit more permanent. Can we just capture this intense moment? Can we stay here in this glimpse into the hidden things of God?

But note what they've been talking about. Jesus is talking with Moses and Elijah about his "departure." The Greek word here is a form of "exodus." Jesus is about to accomplish his exodus at Jerusalem. We'd love to know what the conversation was like, of course. Was Jesus sharing strategy, or were Moses and Elijah encouraging him? Or was there something else happening?

The word "exodus" here is not to be missed, however. It is critical for us to learn something about the crucifixion itself and all that goes with it. Luke and the rest of the New Testament writers draw a specific, explicit parallel between the Exodus in the Old Testament and what Jesus accomplishes in the New. Jesus' crucifixion is about freedom. He breaks the chains of our bondage. He gives us a new identity. He defeats the powers spiritual and secular. He takes us through death into new life. He refers to his own death as a baptism. His resurrection conquers the power of death and prepares a way for us to live with him forever. There are serious parallels here to God leading his people into the Promised Land. This is hardly just normal old Jesus that we've always been used to. Rather, this is a nuclear reaction of God's power to set his people free so that we might live in loving relationship with him and with one another. We get a hint about what the Exodus looks like from God's perspective in Exodus 19. God tells Moses what he has accomplished: he has brought his people out of bondage on eagles' wings and brought them to himself. That is God's agenda for the crucifixion of Jesus and his resurrection as well. He sets us free and brings us to himself. This is the essence of the kingdom Jesus came to proclaim, the new wineskins we've been watching him enact all along. This promise is not some future heaven that only happens after we die, but an intimate relationship with God that begins here and now. If we let it, his gracious kingship transforms our spiritual lives and our daily relationships. There's nothing humdrum about this.

Questions to think about:
1. What would you say is the most awe-inspiring thing you've ever experienced personally?
2. How do you think people get jaded to the amazing message of Jesus, of Christianity?
3. Have you ever been asked to tell someone who you think Jesus is? What happened?
4. How is Jesus' crucifixion a parallel to the Exodus in the Old Testament?

Luke 9:37-50

The contrast between the mount of transfiguration and the situation that confronts Jesus, Peter, James and John when they come down from the mountain is striking. Jesus is thrust back into the middle of a hurting, broken world that needs his attention. The glory of the mountaintop becomes a dim memory all too quickly. Oswald Chambers, in one of his excellent devotions (July 6) in the book *My Utmost for His Highest*, says that we receive the vision on the mountaintop but immediately we are brought into the valley to be beaten into shape to receive the vision. There is a great deal of truth in that insight as you read through the verses following Luke's account of the transfiguration. If you have ever been in a situation where God has given you a vision of his will for you, you might well identify: We want to go right from the mountain to the ascension, but there is suffering and crucifixion to endure first.

It's easy to get discouraged if God brings you into that kind of a season, and it's easy to become self-focused in that meantime. We see the disciples doing exactly this: they cannot cast out the demon in the boy, in spite of Jesus' earlier commission to them (9:1-6). Jesus is still the one who possesses "majesty" (v. 43) that astonishes the crowd!

Jesus reminds the disciples what he has told them before: He will go to Jerusalem, be arrested and crucified. But again, the disciples are unready (unlike Moses and Elijah on the mountain) to get their minds around the vision of what God is doing. They fall into an argument about which of them wields the most power. Jesus gives them an alternative way of thinking about power, a way that echoes Psalm 131. A child, quietly confident in the love of the parent, is to be their example.

The disciples still don't get it: Now they try to exercise control over another preacher. Jesus again offers a different way of seeing. The one who is not actively opposing him is with him. Jesus will contradict these words in a different context (see 11:23) but here the meaning is clear: Like Paul in Philippians 1:15-18, Jesus recognizes that God is at work in a wider context. What's more, God isn't concerned to make sure his trademark and his branding is stamped on all the work he is doing. Fact is, if something glorifies God, it will also glorify Jesus, and he is remarkably openhanded about that.

The example of Jesus here is one of patience and trust. He knows that God will accomplish his will. He also knows it will be a difficult road. Part of what God is doing in the meantime is training up the disciples. He is giving them the critically important experience of following Jesus to the cross. This journey to Jerusalem (9:51ff) will transform what they think about who Jesus is and what it means to follow him. God is hammering them into shape to receive the vision.

Questions to think about:
1. What emotions were the disciples feeling after the transfiguration? What clues do you see in the text?
2. Have you ever received a promise from God, but then you had to wait? What was that like?
3. Reflect on how Jesus redefines power and authority for the disciples. What are your thoughts?
4. Is it easy for you to let others do things their own way, or are you prone to control things? Explain.

Luke 9:51-62

Verse 51 is the watershed of Luke's narrative. Up to this point Jesus has been establishing his public ministry, demonstrating who he is and thus who God is. He does this by acting to heal, to preach, to cast out demons, to associate with the lowly and the broken. Now he sets his face to go to Jerusalem. The cross is waiting, and Jesus goes to make sure the plan of God is enacted in its fullness. Now that the character, identity, and kingship of

God has been revealed on earth through Jesus' ministry, people are accountable for their judgment of Jesus. They will reject him. In the end even the Twelve forsook him and fled. So the cross, where God takes our rebellion and brokenness into himself and forgives us, is the necessary outworking of God's love. God will stop at nothing to have a relationship with you.

One of the things that is hard for us to understand is that Jesus is the most authentic person possible. He is utterly true to himself and his character at all times. Most of us live lives in which we deceive ourselves and others about the truth of our character, but Jesus never does this. Jesus' authenticity is the reason why people reject him. The Samaritan village rejects Jesus because it is clear he is going to Jerusalem. (There was a significant argument going back 900 years, evident in Jesus' conversation with the woman at the well in John 4, about which was the appropriate place to worship—Jerusalem or Samaria.) Jesus' face is set toward Jerusalem, and the Samaritans will not accept him.

The three individuals in the end of Luke 9 provide cryptic yet cautionary examples to us. Their discipleship apparently ends before it begins. In the first case, the potential follower is eager and ready to commit, and Jesus says (as he says elsewhere), "Count the cost." What does it mean to jump into this life with Jesus? We don't know, but the text implies that this person doesn't choose to follow a rabbi who has nowhere to lay his head.

The next one is called by Jesus but the constraints of this person's family of origin outweigh Jesus' call. While it sounds in English as though the father was probably dead and awaiting the funeral–a matter of just a few hours or at most days–culturally, it's very possible that the father was aging but nowhere near dead. This could represent years of putting off the choice to follow Jesus. Jesus responds with what sounds like a lack of compassion, but his incisive comment cuts to the heart of the person's idolatry of family over following Jesus.

The third individual is similar, but just wants to say farewell to family. Jesus names this person's "looking back" and says that kind of obsession with the past will be debilitating to his followers. In farming, plowing a straight furrow requires picking a spot on the far side of the field and steadily working toward it. If one is constantly looking over their shoulder, the furrow will zig-zag all over the place. We are called to keep our eyes on Jesus (Hebrews 12:1-2) and work for his kingship and his glory. Some of us are so obsessed with the sins of the past–our own or others'–that we make little progress toward future goals.
Self-awareness is different from past-focus.

In each of these cases, it is the lordship of Jesus that is at stake. Each individual seeks to compromise their commitment to Jesus' lordship in some significant way. Jesus says what he does not because of a lack of compassion. Rather, he knows that his lordship in each of these people's lives is the very best possible thing for them. He will not compromise his own character to make the following easier.

It is so easy for us to be inauthentic. We shape our stories, telling only the comfortable parts to each individual we encounter. It is so hard to be honest about uncomfortable truths. If we dare to tell a more authentic version of our own story, we allow our hearers to self-select. Some will choose to "unfriend" us. Others will choose to reengage in a deeper way.

Looking ahead, what happens to those who will follow this absolutely authentic Jesus, even though it is difficult? We'll see in chapter 10 that they will be sent out in the joy of serving Jesus and proclaiming his kingship even as he marches onward toward the cross.

Questions to think about:
1. Does it surprise you that people reject Jesus? Why / Why not?
2. What does it mean that Jesus is the most authentic person ever?
3. Which of the three potential disciples at the end of chapter 9 is most like you? Why?
4. Why is authenticity hard for us?

Luke 10:1-24

I have been running up against the difference lately between authority and power.

Satan undeniably has power. He has power to destroy in so many devastating ways. He has power to prevent growth. Picture the most devastating kinds of relational damage. The heroin addict that compromises and betrays every relationship, for the sake of an addiction; the marriage that can never quite get past defensiveness, self pity, and fear; the parent who over-indulges their child and prevents them from growing strong and vibrant; the fearful lover (or parent or boss or teacher or ...) whose insecurity demands rigid control of the one who should be loved and set free.

All of these examples (and of course there are thousands more) demonstrate power exercised without, or in contravention of, legitimate authority. (FWIW, control is always at odds with love.) And whether demonic forces are directly involved or not, each of these thousands of examples are exactly what Jesus described in John 10: The thief comes to steal, kill, and destroy the abundant life God longs to give his creation.

I spent a few hours yesterday afternoon cutting buckthorn. There's a beautiful trail back in the woods east of my place that has been choked by the invasive, tangly stuff. At one time it was a wild, remote haven for people to pull in their RVs and camp in the isolation of a beautiful woods. Buckthorn has closed off the trails, cramped the campsites, and choked out native species. So I got my pole trimmer out and spent a couple hours clearing one specific trail. It felt a little like spitting in the wind, but it's probably better than just letting the awful stuff grow without protest. Buckthorn has no authority to be here. It's an invasive species and everybody agrees it's bad, but it has tremendous power. Left unchecked it will dominate a plot of land and completely take over.

Jesus doesn't give his followers a lot of power. But he does give them authority. And when, after exercising that authority (v. 17) the disciples are pumped up on what they perceive as their power, Jesus reminds them that it is authority he has given.

Satan has no authority unless we invite him in. Unless we agree with his lies, he has no right to exercise his power over us. He will certainly try, but we can stand in our rightful identity as children of God. We remind Satan that we are bought by the blood of Jesus, and in spite of our weakness, claim the authority of Jesus himself. It's an important distinction. We most often measure ourselves based on our perception of power, but God's word makes clear that he values our weakness (see 2 Corinthians 12). In some way, Jesus delights to exercise his power as we stand, utterly defenseless, in his authority that he has given us.

One of the most vivid examples of this is the apocalyptic battle in Revelation 19, sometimes described as the "battle of Armageddon." The name really just refers to a plain in the north of Israel that was a famous battleground in ancient times. In the account in Revelation 19, all the armies of light and darkness line up, prepared to do battle, clashing swords against shields, shouting battle cries, scavenger birds circling overhead. But the battle is decided when Jesus rides out on his horse and speaks a word (that's the sword that comes out of his mouth, in

Revelation's obscure imagery) and defeats all the battalions of hell. In other words, we're there, we're at the battle site, but we're just spectators. Cheerleaders. We don't exercise power, Jesus does.

This is a game changer. What does it mean to stand in your identity and authority as a child of God today? What does it mean to really believe a) that God calls you his beloved son or daughter in whom he is well pleased, and b) that he gives you authority to stand against all the forces of hell, implicit and explicit? This is worth pondering. This gets right to the heart of what it means for us to proclaim what Jesus called "the kingdom of God."

Questions to think about:
1. Think about the news coverage you see. Is it usually more focused on power or authority?
2. How does Satan work to steal, kill, and destroy the joy God desires to create in relationships?
3. Why do you think God seems so eager to be present in our weakness?
4. What would it mean to stand today in the authority Jesus gives you?

Luke 10:25-37

Probably no other parable has been more effectively turned into a morality tale than this one that we usually call "The Good Samaritan." We assume Jesus is saying, "You should be nice to people, especially hurting people, and especially those who are different from you." While this is not a bad lesson, Jesus is up to something much deeper here than just a cautionary tale of "be nice." Remember that from its outset, Jesus' conversation with the lawyer is about the law. Jesus helps the lawyer articulate the basic message of the law: love God and love your neighbor. So far so good.

The rub comes in that the lawyer, Luke makes very clear, wants to "justify himself." The word in Greek here is another form of the same word Paul uses so often, for example in Romans 3:20. Paul here states unequivocally that no one will be justified through works of the law. It would be dangerous to assume Jesus is preaching a message of "be nice and you shall be justified." We would then have to say the rest of the New Testament preaches against that very understanding. How can we make sense of this?

The theological distinction between Law and Gospel is helpful here. Many theologians have articulated this distinction, but its roots go right back to the New Testament. Jesus takes us on a surprising journey to get the lawyer's eyes off the Law and turn him to the Gospel.

So what does Jesus do with the lawyer's question?

Jesus' move here is surprising. Ask yourself the question, who is the Christ figure in the parable? Who is most like Jesus? Most often we assume that the Samaritan is the Christ figure. He's obviously the hero, after all. However, there's no real justification for this assumption in the parable. By contrast, there are several reasons to say that Jesus draws a clear parallel between himself and the wounded man. The language he uses to describe the man's experience, for one. The man fell among robbers, who stripped him and beat him and departed. This is very much what will happen to Jesus in the coming days. He will be arrested by those who come at night like robbers, convicted by an illegal court, beaten by his own people and then by the Romans, and crucified between two robbers. He will be rejected by the priests and Levites, the religious authorities of his people. And he will be left for dead.

If the wounded man is the Christ figure in the story, suddenly a few things pop. Notably, the priest and the Levite both judge themselves by their reaction to Jesus. The Samaritan judges himself as well by his sympathy and his care. It's interesting to view this parable in light of Jesus' teachings in Matthew 25 about the sheep and the goats, about those who have recognized him in the needy among them. "I was hungry and you fed me," Jesus says. Jesus, the Crucified One, is the judge of the world. Or, as we've said before, the world judges itself by its response to Jesus. Jesus exercises this judgment in the surprising way of being wounded, beaten, killed, and raised. He is a scandalous Savior, an offensive Messiah. Only those who have been outcast themselves–like the Samaritan–are likely to respond favorably to him.

Jesus (as John writes) came into his own–his own creation, his own people, his own homeland–and his own "received him not." The Samaritan, by contrast, is one who receives Jesus (the Wounded One), builds his life and his actions around Jesus, and expends his resources for Jesus' sake. Those who are currently in power (priests and Levites, for example) are less likely to expend themselves in such a way. The outcasts are more likely to live out Jesus' own compassion and mercy for others. Jesus is, in this parable and in every way, the Wounded Savior, the Crucified Messiah.

Questions to think about:
1. When you were a child, who taught you to be nice to others? How did they teach this?
2. What is the difference between "being nice" and putting your trust in Jesus?
3. What surprises you about this approach to the parable of the Good Samaritan?
4. What is appealing, what is uncomfortable, about seeing Jesus as the Wounded One?

Luke 10:38-11:13

So often we read scripture by chapter and verse divisions, never considering that those structures were not part of the original writings. Chapters were added much later, and verses later yet, as a way to organize the text. They're very helpful, but they limit our thinking too often.

In this text, imagine if the enormous "11" didn't exist on the page. We'd likely read the episode with Mary and Martha at the end of chapter 10 differently. We almost always read this anecdote as its own distinct unit, and almost always we read it as a condemnation of Martha and an endorsement of Mary's devotion. This is satisfying to those who land on the "NF" spectrum of the Meyers-Briggs assessment. If the chapter division was invisible, we would assume that these verses are connected to what immediately follows: the first dozen verses of chapter 11.

Consider the connection points. Martha is concerned with welcoming Jesus into her home as a guest. She is focused on serving, which likely centers on preparing and serving food. In the following verses, Jesus uses the example of a person going to a friend's house to borrow food because a guest has arrived from a journey. Clear connection! Later, near the end of this section, Jesus cites the example of a parent giving their child fish or an egg. Again, concerns about food and serving appropriate food.

Another connection point: After seeing Jesus' interactions with Martha and Mary, and then observing Jesus' own prayer life, the disciples ask specifically for teaching about prayer. (By the way, it's intriguing that Mary and Martha's home is just a short distance from the Garden of Gethsemane on the Mount of Olives east of Jerusalem. It's very possible that the "certain place" of 11:1 is in fact that garden, where we're told elsewhere that Jesus liked to spend time.) It's quite possible that Mary's devotion is part of what spurred the Twelve to ask Jesus about prayer. The prayer that Jesus teaches here (most often called "The Lord's Prayer") is the supreme example of a *disciple's* prayer. It exemplifies Mary's attitude of single-minded submission to the Father through Jesus.

And finally, do not miss the point, well worth digging into, that Jesus sums up all his teaching in this section by saying that the gift the Father is so eager to give is the Holy Spirit (11:13). Jesus is not simply telling the disciples how to communicate with God. Instead, he is encouraging them to seek the one best gift that God has to give: Himself, in the form of his Spirit, residing in the life of the believer. As we begin to know God better and better, we desire him more and more. His answer to this desire is that God gives us his Spirit. This is our truest longing. It goes back to the Garden of Eden where God breathes into us his Spirit, the wind / breath of his own life. This is what we are created for: the indwelling of God's vitality in us. God's Spirit flows in our relationships, loves, passions, creativity, community, devotion, solitude, partnership, work and play.

A couple other things worth noting. N.T. Wright points out that culturally speaking, Mary sitting at Jesus' feet and listening to his teachings was scandalous partly at least because it meant that she was in the men's part of the house, breaking the gender divisions that said women couldn't learn, be disciples, or take part in meaningful discussions and debates. (If you've ever seen the old Barbra Streisand movie "Yentl" you have a sense of this in the Jewish community. It's worth watching.) Over and over again an honest, contextually informed reading of the New Testament (and the Old Testament, for that matter) shatters the cultural limitations that kept women in servitude in those times.

We take our self-centered, post-Enlightenment assumptions and read these words as though they were written for our culture where women have achieved major strides forward in equality and respect. Reading in this way we do violence to scripture. So for example, we read Paul's words that a woman should learn at home in full submission to her husband. We hear that word placing a limit on women, but Paul's original hearers would likely have been shocked by the idea that a woman could learn at all. Paul gives her full access to the intellectual, spiritual, and devotional discussions around the faith, just in a culturally appropriate context.

Jesus is doing a similarly radical thing here. He allows Mary into the conversation, affirms her as an example of appropriate devotion. He calls Martha to recognize the un-health of her own attitudes toward the details, hospitality, and her sister. Jesus radically reinterprets the cultural expectations leveled at the women in his context. Jesus' rhetorical question in 11:13 may very well be a linguistic way to say "those who ask him" implicitly includes the women who were too often swept aside.

So what does one do personally with this story? As I write this, I have been in a "Martha" phase of life, managing details and trying to stay on top of too many spinning plates. Yesterday our church campus was full of kayakers and kids with treasure maps and a bounce house and pulled pork sandwiches and newly installed outdoor speakers playing background music and excellent all-beef hotdogs over the bonfire. Lots of moving parts, lots of preparation, lots of Martha-like "serving" in a multiplicity of ways. Then yesterday evening I led the final training session with a ministry team before we launch next

Sunday. This group of a couple dozen leaders are dear partners in adventure, launching into something that feels bigger than what we can manage. At least three times during last night's training, I said, "Don't worry about the horses, just load the wagon." So often if we are living by God's Spirit, in that pneumanaut (i.e., Spirit-driven) sailing that he calls us to do, we have to plan in such a way that if God doesn't show up we will look utterly foolish. We are extending as fully as we can, yearning for God to do the work that only he can do. We know that if he doesn't show up, we will look foolish and be bitterly disappointed.

That's why Jesus' words toward the end of this section are so critically important. We're not asking for a scorpion or a snake. We are asking for good gifts. God loves to show up and do what only he can do. Jesus promises that if we lift him up, he will use us to draw people to himself. In the process, even our potentially disappointed trust becomes a witness to the goodness of God himself. How much more will he pour out his Spirit, giving the good gift of himself to his children?

Even in the midst of a life consumed by details, there are potent reminders of the provision, power, and love of God. Life is full, and good, and intense. I need to remember to stop, to breathe, to sit at Jesus' feet. I need to ask him for his Spirit. He loves to give that best of gifts, and so many other good gifts that go with a life lived in love and submission to him.

Questions to think about:
1. Are you more like Mary, or like Martha? What is it like for you to read about these two sisters?
2. How does the Lord's Prayer provide a good picture of Mary's devotion?
3. How are we doing these days with empowering women and others who have been marginalized?
4. What does it mean for you to hear that God loves to give you good gifts, especially his Spirit?

Luke 11:14-26

It sometimes seems quaint and medieval to believe that there is a spiritual world around us peopled with personalities and powers. Jesus, however, took seriously the idea of a very real spiritual world and the powers that inhabit it.

Many of us come at these biblical stories of the demonic with a first-grade-level simplistic view. We start out believing that there is a Real, physical world. That's reality in our minds. Then we believe that there's a heaven "up there" and a hell "down there." But those are substantially less "real" to us. When we grow in our understanding of the Bible these spatial imaginings start to seem unreasonable. The first Russian cosmonauts in orbit triumphantly proclaimed that there was no heaven and no God, thus defeating the entire worldview of Christianity. But their simplistic claim didn't shake the faith of many believers.

As we grow deeper into a biblical worldview, we start to understand that "heaven" in scripture refers not simply to a place we go when we die. Rather, it summarizes that unseen spiritual realm where God's power reigns supreme. Heaven in this sense (or maybe more accurately "the heavens") is parallel to and accessible from this reality. The final book of the Bible is a "revelation" because it pulls aside the curtain so we might catch a glimpse into reality seen from God's point of view. We get to see into the heavens.

It is interesting to talk with those from any part of the world who practice primal religions (shamanism and various forms of animism). There is a surprising unity to their systems of belief that is, in fact, hard to explain without some basis in reality. Almost without exception, shamans will tell you that the physical and the spiritual realities are interwoven. So there are spiritual realities to the trees, and the swamps, and the hills. There are "thin places" in this world where the spiritual world is more accessible. Not all of the spiritual powers are seeking our good. They can be bribed, cajoled, manipulated, paid off. But they are malicious and dangerous. These spiritual realities can harm and inhabit and oppress human beings. In fact, according to these "primal" religions we live in the midst of a tangled mess of spiritual realities. In many ways we are at their mercy, if in fact they had any. According to the shamans, these spiritual powers are not all-powerful, not at all. The spirits themselves live in fear of other powers, snarling and snapping at one another like stray dogs. We, in turn, are like foxes living in a forest: We have some powers of our own, but we are vulnerable to the larger predators.

This is the world that undergirds every one of the major religions. Each of these major religions dresses up these basic spiritual realities. Each develops systems and views to deal with these experienced, intuited cosmologies. Buddhism says it's all an illusion; Hinduism says that all those spiritual powers are in fact gods, millions of them, and one needs to learn to live in harmony with all of them. Shintoism says that one needs allies in the spiritual world, and in fact one's own ancestors are the best allies. Judaism, Christianity, and Islam all claim the revelation of a supreme God who is supreme over all the spiritual powers. The existence of a supreme God in each of these religions does not negate the reality of the spiritual world.

Jesus himself functioned as though this shamanic worldview was quite real and present. This is why over and over again in the gospels, the marvel is not his power to heal, but his authority over the spiritual world. To this day in well over half the world, Jesus' demonstrated power over the spiritual world is a compelling reason for people to surrender to him as Lord. Many people become followers of Jesus for their own spiritual protection.

If we do not have at least some kind of sense of the spiritual world as real and accessible, much of the gospels will seem pointless. But the powers are there, as Jesus repeatedly demonstrates.

How do we then live with this view? The key, of course, is to know Jesus and remain close to him, to take the New Testament seriously when it says that Jesus has authority over these other powers. It is not enough to know about Jesus, as the exorcists in Acts 19 discovered. His name is not a magic formula. His authority is relational. He himself is the stronger man who beats and robs Satan, even when Satan has bolted his doors and trusts in the strength of his rebellion.

The spiritual dimension works itself out into the mundane details of our lives in the least surprising ways. The ongoing argument between husband and wife that simply can't move forward for some reason; the way we surround ourselves with cloaks of invulnerability, protecting our hearts and refusing to truly love; the snide spread of gossip that alienates people and propagates prejudice... All of these are the outworkings of the spiritual world. C.S. Lewis has done an amazing job of portraying these realities in his classic *The Screwtape Letters*.

When we refuse the God-given gifts of love, joy, and peace because of our own fears, we make tacit agreements with the spiritual powers. They oppose the life God alone can give. These agreements begin to work together into systems of injustice that routinely destroy lives and prevent abundance. And this is why all our political railing and our human protests, however justified, are powerless to make changes. We lack the authority to command the spiritual world, unless we are acting in and explicitly by the name of Jesus. It's relational.

Jesus is not telling cute stories here. He is describing an unseen but very real aspect of our own condition. In this as in every dimension of life, he is our only hope.

Questions to think about:
1. What do you think about the reality of invisible spiritual powers existing around us?
2. How does Jesus demonstrate his authority over these unseen spiritual powers?
3. Why should we understand that the spiritual realm is both parallel to and accessible from our reality?
4. How have you seen the influence of spiritual powers in your own life and relationships?

Luke 11:27-54

This whole section, in a variety of ways, develops and explicates Jesus' words to the woman: "Blessed rather are those who hear the word of God and keep it!" Like every other generation, ours is tempted to make Christianity a matter of external obedience. We turn Jesus' movement into a system of behavior modification. We strive to keep issues like repentance and law and righteousness outside our cores. As long as I can keep these things away from the deepest part of me, I can feel good about myself. So we strive to be good, and we judge those who fall short in our eyes of what we think 'being good' looks like. Please understand that this is not Christianity. It is what a friend of mine calls "the gospel of sin management." Every religion in the world practices some sort of sin management. Managing our behavior is necessary. But don't miss this:

when Jesus judges this world, one of the first things he judges is religion.

This is why so many supposedly Christian congregations are little more than feel-good institutions built on tribalism and shame. Tribalism, because if we can make sure everyone who comes in looks like us and behaves like us, we feel good. Shame because when someone breaks our boundaries, we first judge them, then gossip about them, shun them, and finally exclude them. We are no better than the generation to which Jesus spoke, saying that the blood of all the prophets from Abel to Zechariah would fall on them. The prophets brought a message of heart transformation that impacted external actions. In other words, get right with God at your core and let him straighten out your works. But that message is too threatening to us because it demands that we stop seeing ourselves as already justified. If we take that message to heart, we must stop seeing ourselves as already "in."

Jesus makes a big deal of the example of Jonah. Consider that story for a moment. These days most of what's written about Jonah deals with its historicity. Could a large fish in fact swallow a man, and could a man live for three days inside a fish? That's the question that occupies us as post-Enlightenment readers. So you can read about large groupers that have been found in the Mediterranean and apocryphal stories of sailors who were swallowed by this or that fish and later found alive. Our minds totally miss the point, just as Jesus' own generation did. If you read the story of Jonah carefully, it has little to do with the fish. The story is an indictment of the Israelites' own selfish attitudes toward their enemies. Commanded by God to be a light to the people of Nineveh, Jonah flees the opposite direction. Jonah is corrected by God through storm and fish. Along the way he incidentally serves as a powerful witness to the sailors. He finally, reluctantly, goes to Nineveh, preaches the worst sermon in history, and witnesses an amazing revival. The Assyrians turn en masse toward God. And Jonah is furious, because he knew God would find a reason to be merciful to these people Jonah despises.

We rarely talk about the end of Jonah's story, but it encapsulates the whole point. Jonah sits outside the city of Nineveh, hoping to watch the fire-and-brimstone show, but instead he sees God act in mercy. Jonah is hot out there on the hillside in the sun, so he's deeply thankful when a vine grows up that provides shade for him. But then a cutworm comes along and kills the vine and it withers, taking away Jonah's shade. He begins to curse because the vine is dead. God speaks to him and asks, are you angry for the vine? Yes, Jonah says, you bet I am, angry enough to die. God uses Jonah's selfish concern for the vine as a way to help Jonah understand: God is concerned for the people of Nineveh, and even for its cattle. You get the impression that the little mini-sermon God preaches at the end of the book probably flew right over Jonah's head. Jonah remains stuck in his selfishness and tribalism. As long as he can keep viewing the Ninevites as the enemy, he can feel good about himself. He's in, and the Assyrians are out.

Jesus confronts the people around him with this same kind of word. The Pharisees and teachers of the law excelled at evaluating the conduct of the people around them. They were the guardians of public morality. Jesus says, it's more than that. It's about the attitude of your heart. This at its core is what it means to "hear the word of God and keep it." The word of God calls us to see God alone as righteous. We are sinful, broken people who need mercy. Those who know God and his loving character are not those who have somehow arrived so they can sit in judgment over others; rather, those who know God and his loving character become like one beggar telling another where to find bread.

We always want to become the hero of the story. We want to be the Good Guy. But the gospel makes clear that we are so far from that status. Jesus alone is the Good Guy. His character is love. His character is mercy. That which reflects his character—love, wholeness, self-sacrifice, inspiration, beauty—is affirmed by his gospel. That which opposes Jesus' love and mercy is condemned. All of this starts in the heart. Christianity is never a "fake it till you make it" religion; it is a broken-hearted relationship with a loving Jesus. He brings us to a healing and wholeness that is dependent not on our own behavior modification, but on his goodness and love.

Questions to think about:
1. Why is it so tempting for us to sit in judgment on the behavior of others?
2. How well do you know the story of Jonah? Does the description here fit what you know?

3. What is the difference between faith that starts in the heart and works outward, versus religion that starts with changing outward action?
4. What do you think are forces that oppose Jesus' love and mercy in our own day?

Luke 12:1-12

Once again, like it was a theme, Jesus confronts those who would create their own religion on the basis of sin management. He rejects their distorted focus out of hand.

Notice that this conversation happens in the context of Jesus' amazing success. People are coming by the thousands, even trampling each other, to see Jesus. He has attained rock star status. Whenever spiritual leaders of any stripe become successful, there is a tremendous pressure–internal and external–to cut corners. In the words of Jonas Nightingale in the excellent movie "Leap of Faith" the public religious figure must "always look better than they do." As soon as we focus on appearances, we begin to hide the less-than-comfortable details from ourselves and from others. We lie to ourselves and others in a thousand little ways. This is a tragically common story in the world of religious leadership. Not only high profile leaders, but everyone who participates in the oxymoron of organized religion faces this temptation.

This is why shame is such a powerful tool. Nearly everyone is hiding something. The story is told of Sir Arthur

Conan Doyle, the author of the Sherlock Holmes stories, sending an anonymous telegram to ten top-level officials in the British government. The telegram simply read, "All is discovered. Flee at once." Within twenty-four hours, every one of the officials had left the country. Doyle didn't know any damning details about these officials, but he understood human nature. We live in fear that the abysmal truth about us will be discovered, that people will see us naked and ashamed.

This fear gives religion its power. Shame is a powerful motivational tool, but deep down we recognize that it is wrong and unhealthy to be motivated in this way.

Jesus speaks to our fear. Verses 4-7 deserve a much closer reading than they usually receive. Jesus says multiple times that we should fear God rather than humans. He says this so explicitly (verse 5) that it seems obvious. But then (verse 6) Jesus says a couple of really odd things: sparrows are cheap. The hairs on your head are numbered. In other words, the God whom you fear, the God who is going to Get You for Being Bad, doesn't want to Get You at all. God cares for the throwaway birds. God is attentive to each hair that washes down the drain of your shower. So what?

So don't be afraid.

Wait a minute! Jesus just said we should fear God. Now he says don't be afraid. What? That's exactly the point. All our shame-based systems assume that God is judging us and finding us lacking. We assume that people are watching, evaluating, judging. And perhaps they are, but their opinions, believe it or not, don't matter. God is both attentive and loving, though we find it hard to believe. Fear not.

Jesus moves on to his trump card, consistent with what he has been preaching all along: He is the authorized representative of God. He is the anointed Messiah, the one and only Son of God with authority over all creation. He is the one who has been eating with tax collectors, drinking with sinners, anointed by a prostitute. He has come not to condemn but to love. He has come to break down the hypocritical systems of shame. And even if we mistake him, if we badmouth him, he forgives, just as he will do from the cross. But the Spirit-driven reality of God is the one who helps us truly understand who God is. It is the Spirit who helps us see Jesus. In seeing him clearly, we see the Father. God help us if we close ourselves off to this revelation.

Lots to ponder.

So take a break from the ponderous and chuckle with me for a moment at a memory: Bible college, a million years ago, and a big exam in one of our classes. I asked a friend how much he had studied, and he said, "Not a bit. I'm going to Luke 12:12 this one."

Not sure that is what Jesus was talking about—my friend failed the exam—but it still makes me laugh.

Questions to think about:
1. How much do you compare yourself to others? Do you think this is healthy or unhealthy? Why?
2. What does it feel like to have someone really pay attention to you?
3. What does it mean to "fear God"?
4. How does Jesus accurately represent God's love? What does that mean for us?

Luke 12:13-34

I am not by nature an anxious person, but I've dipped my toe into those frantic waters a time or two and have tasted just how precarious an anxious life can be. My own temperament is not to be actively fearful about what might happen; instead I tend toward an Eeyore depressive streak. I look at the great things I long for or the massive tragedies I fear and get morose about a future that is less joyful or more painful than I desire. I know many people who live in a heightened state of anxiety, however, and I feel for that fearful state of existence. It's rough to see someone you love in that edge-of-panic place.

Jesus gives us clear direction regarding anxiety.

I don't know the statistics, but I have heard that our society has become more and more anxious over the past few decades. I wonder about that. I wonder about our expectations, both our desires and our fears. How much anxiety is rooted in the fact that we have instant access to tragedies all over the globe? Our own circumstances become colored by that fearful knowledge. On the other hand, how much anxiety is rooted in the fact that we are constantly bombarded with messages about what we could have, how good our lives could be? These messages are by definition an illusion based on someone else's agenda to influence us. Yet these messages communicate to us that we are not enough.

Whether it is my depressive tendencies or the anxious churning of someone I love, I believe so much of this comes down to the internal voices in our own souls that point toward fear, and disappointment. Perhaps this gets near the core of the problem. Maybe we are apt to listen to the wrong voices, and maybe this is where Jesus can speak in the imperative, "Do not be anxious." He is directing us to be careful about which voices we heed.

This section starts with a story of a man who is too obviously listening to the voices of his own baseless confidence. His treasure is focused on himself and his own wealth that provides some insulation against difficult tomorrows. He desires treasure for his own sake, not as an expression or an outgrowth of God's rule in his life. The difference is monumental. It is the difference between worship and idolatry.

After this caricature, Jesus gets to the meat of the necessary attitude change: Don't be anxious, don't listen to the voices of scarcity or deprivation or tragedy. (He will deal more explicitly with tragedy in the next chapter.) Jesus says first of all that your heavenly Father knows what you need. You need food and clothing, of course. By extension you also need the higher levels of old Maslow's hierarchy. So love, meaningful work, a sense of agency, partnership in that work, and the ability to shape the world around you are important as well. Your Father knows you need these things.

The Bible does not claim that the believer's life will be pain-free. Far from it. Hebrews 12 is a good example of a healthy attitude toward the sometimes painful challenges of life. God allows these factors in our lives that discipline us toward strength. If you've ever dealt with a spoiled child, you know firsthand why this is so important to God! But the Bible points to a loving God who provides good gifts to his children.

Second, Jesus advises us to seek God's kingdom. The trouble with the wealthy man in Jesus' parable at the beginning of this section is that he was seeking his own kingdom. Seek God's rule and God's glorification over this good creation, Jesus says, and let God take care of the details.

Jesus ends this section with the ultimate response to our seeking the kingship of God: He says don't be afraid: It is your Father's good pleasure to give you the kingdom. In other words, set out to seek the kingdom of God in every area of your life. Seek God's rule in your relationships, work, management of resources, the clothes you wear and the food you eat. It may well be that as you seek these things, God will break down some of the systems in your life. Your diet may need to change if God is king over it.

You may start shopping at different stores, or shopping considerably less, if your focus is on the kingdom. There may be relationships in your life that are so far from what God intends that they will need to be broken for the sake of his kingship. Treasure this sovereignty of a loving God. He longs for you to live in this kind of trust. Submit your longings to him, and he will supply the treasures you long for in his good timing.

Such a view of life is far, far from what the newscasts or the advertisers would have you living. Perhaps a life lived seeking God's kingship will mean decreasing your exposure to both advertising and news broadcasts.

The whole time I've been writing this post, a young woodchuck has been grazing in my front yard. I've seen him frequently these last couple weeks. He's a good example to me of exactly what Jesus describes in this passage. God has richly provided for his needs here in my yard. He has few predators, ample food, a secure hole not far back in the woods to the south. It's not a perfect life, but it's a very good one, and God deserves the credit for all of that. Recognizing God's good provision and thanking him for it is appropriate. It might be a good step away from both anxiety and depression.

Questions to think about:
1. How much do you experience either anxiety or depression?
2. It's easy to dislike the wealthy man in the parable. How much are we like him?

3. To what extent do we really believe that God simply wants us to be happy?
4. What would it look like in your life this week to let your treasures be under God's kingly rule?

Luke 12:35-59

Jesus builds here on the theme he has been stating and restating throughout Luke's gospel. Most recently he states it in verse 24: "Where your treasure is, there your heart will be also." The clear idea is that *Jesus* is to be our treasure. He generously gives us all kinds of other gifts. He gives us work for his kingdom and partnerships toward that work. He provides the gifts of human relationships, loving bonds that are a joy in themselves and point us toward him. But Jesus is and remains the supreme goal and focus of our faith. That's the launching point for what we often take to be a dire prediction of the future.

But Jesus is not speaking of the future in these verses. He is speaking to the present reality of his situation and that of his hearers. Apply Jesus' words first and foremost to his original context, and imagine how his listeners would have heard them. (We are so quick to make ourselves the immediate focus of scripture!) Jesus is the master coming home. He will very shortly dress himself for service and wash his disciples' feet. He will be poured out, his body and blood given for them on the cross. When he says "The Son of Man is coming at an hour you do not expect," he is in effect asking if they recognize him, standing before them. "Here I am!" The verses that follow are an indictment of the current authorities over the Jews: Herod, Pilate, Caiaphas. All these are included in the description in verses 45-46. His words are reminiscent of the prophets, notably Ezekiel 34 where God speaks to indict the shepherds of his people. Jesus speaks in a kind of code, which is always the function of apocalyptic speech and writing in the Bible. What sounds to outsiders like dire predictions of a science-fiction-style future are actually clear messages about current realities to the insider.

Jesus' message as he goes on bears this out. His followers are walking immediately into a situation in which their people will be divided over Jesus and his message. His followers will become estranged within a generation or two from their Jewish families. The war that ended with the destruction of Jerusalem in 70 AD drove the final nails in the coffin that divided Christian from Jew.

Verses 54-56 tell us clearly that Jesus is speaking not of some distant apocalyptic future, but to his present moment. He says so in so many words. The key message is that his hearers fail to recognize Jesus for who he really is.

So what are we, two thousand years later, to do with this passage? As we'll see in chapter 13, the message for us is fairly simple: What do we do with Jesus? How do we react to him? Our options are simple: reject him or surrender to him. In essence we are not so different from Peter and John, or Herod and Caiaphas for that matter. We may be indifferent to Jesus, or admirers who want to use him for our own ends. Or we may consider him our supreme treasure and lose all else to find him.

Oswald Chambers wrote, "Watch when God shifts your circumstances, and see whether you are going with Jesus or siding with the world, the flesh and the devil." Following Jesus often looks very different than we think it does. He may call us to follow into difficulty, alienation, and loneliness. These things are not the goal, but they are sometimes the temporary consequences of following him faithfully. The only way this makes sense is if we are keeping our eyes focused on Jesus, trusting that he will lead us into good pastures (Psalm 37). Then when he engineers our circumstances, he is working not just for his kingdom and his glory but also for our good within it.

Questions to think about:
1. How easy is it for you to try to imagine how Jesus' original hearers would receive his words?
2. Do you think we still fail to recognize Jesus for who he is? Explain.
3. How does God change the circumstances of our lives? Have you experienced this lately?
4. What would it mean this week to let Jesus be your treasure?

Luke 13:1-9

Luke 13 is an uncomfortable chapter. Jesus starts out addressing one of the perennial questions posed to religion: Where is God, and what is he up to, when bad things happen? The Roman governor, Pilate, had killed some Jews while they were worshiping in the Temple and their blood got mingled with the blood of their sacrifices. To an observant Jew in that day, this was an in-your-face indictment of God. It must have seemed like God was not watching out for his faithful people. How could this happen? Jesus' response goes far beyond the specific example. "Unless you repent, you will all likewise perish." This is not the answer his questioners are looking for! Instead of giving them a theological concept, Jesus gives them a warning. Then he adds another example. This time, instead of abuse of power, Jesus throws in random tragedy. How could a good God allow a tower to collapse on eighteen innocent people? Like Thornton Wilder in his novel *The Bridge of San Luis Rey* we go looking for meaning in tragedy. We hope to find an orderly universe in which the good prosper and the wicked suffer. But that is not what we find. We find a world in which bridges collapse, towers fall, tsunamis devastate seaside villages, seemingly strong marriages collapse, churches decline and die. Life is precarious, and there are no guarantees of safety.

Jesus is not just speaking of the random danger of life, however. He is also directly confronting a nationalistic attitude in his own people. He warns that if his Jewish people continue on their course and miss what God is doing, they will be destroyed as surely as those on whom the tower fell. What is God doing? Look at me, Jesus says over and over. Here I am. God has sent me. Repent and recognize that I am bringing you good news of who God really is, who you really are, and what the truth is about the world around you. Instead of bowing to his authority, the authorities in Jesus' world choose to continue living with their assumptions intact.

Jesus goes on to tell a simple parable: an unfruitful fig tree (a standard Old Testament metaphor for the nation of Israel) is not bearing fruit, so the landowner demands that it be cut down. The gardener asks for a temporary stay. He requests one more year of digging around it and applying manure to see if it will become fruitful.

I've had the opportunity to take down many, many trees. A chainsaw has become one of my regular tools. I know firsthand that removing a tree is a messy process. It seems so terribly destructive. When God allows destruction or tragedy in our lives, it gets messy. But God is faithful, and he is working for his glory and our good. We all want to be perfect, fruitful trees; these are the dreams we imagine for ourselves. That vision takes time—and a lot of manure—to be accomplished. A tree takes time to bear fruit. Life is poured into us ever so slowly.

When rapid changes happen, they may seem like an avalanche. They may feel painfully destructive. At times we can choose change; other times we get caught up in difficult shifts that terrify us. But God is at work. The key, Jesus seems to be saying, is to know God for who he truly is. We need to know his character accurately. It is tempting to look for guarantees. We are all wired to avoid risk.

We need to recognize both who God is and what he is up to. Are we willing to make the hard changes that make abundant life possible? It's a humbling thing, and may require us to face our fears and our weaknesses in ways we never wanted to. The only reason to choose such risk is if we believe that God is, as Jesus says, love, and that God's love is the ultimate reality. God will sweep away rulers and structures and churches and relationships that don't reflect his love for this world. Have no fear, little flock, for it is your Father's good pleasure to give you the kingdom.

Questions to think about:
1. Have you ever asked why bad things happen? What was that questioning like for you?
2. How does Jesus' response—warning us that we must repent—make you feel?
3. What situations might be described as God destroying things in us that are unfruitful?
4. What is one place in your life this week where you need to surrender to God's loving rule?

Luke 13:10-20

Again in this text we see Jesus reaching out in his authority. Again he demonstrates God's love to a person who would have been considered a throwaway by her society. This woman has been bound for eighteen years, and no doubt her disability had reduced her tangible value to the people around her. *Oh, her? She can't do much. She's so bent over and crippled up. Poor woman.* Their pity masks the fact that they have thoroughly devalued her. Jesus sees her not as a poor crippled woman deserving of pity, but as a daughter of Abraham afflicted unjustly by Satan these past eighteen years. Because it seems so far outside their abilities to heal her, they have written her off. Jesus, on the other hand, frees her and restores her place and her dignity.

I preached once on this text in a tiny Presbyterian church in Jordan, Montana, among people who knew horses. I borrowed an old set of hobbles from a rancher and used them to illustrate what Jesus is talking about in this text. What do hobbles do? They bind a horse, limit its movement, impede its freedom. God created horses for speed, grace, and strength. Hobbles limit all of that.

What are your hobbles? What are the factors that keep you from being all God created you to be? This is a hard question, and often uncomfortable to explore. Maybe they are obvious, like this woman's physical disability. Maybe they are more subtle, like a secret addiction or a struggle with depression. Maybe your hobbles masquerade as a good thing like a servant heart, or an overabundance of empathy.

I've been wrestling lately with something a counselor told me a year and a half ago. He said, "You're so focused on being nice. You get a lot of your identity from being a nice person. Don't get me wrong, kindness to others and compassion for others' failings are good qualities. But you're so nice that you're not really nice. You don't set up any boundaries and people just run right over you." Au contraire, I thought, you should see the boundaries I have set up... and quickly I ran through a bunch of examples in my head. But as we talked further, I realized there were a couple relationships close to my heart where I had allowed others to set my limits. Jeff, you can never shut down a conversation. You can never hang up the phone no matter how angry I'm making you. You can never postpone hard conversations. You can never point out my faults. You can never contradict me.

I was hobbled. Because I was raised to be a nice Minnesota boy who was kind and caring and avoided conflict, I allowed my boundaries to be stolen. I had promised myself that I would never walk away from hard things, and somehow that got twisted in my heart to mean I could never say, "Enough." No matter how badly I wanted to, I couldn't set a firm limit.

I've been processing those hobbles lately. I've had a lot of time to ponder what kindness actually looks like in practice. I'm letting Jesus bring those things to light. It's a challenging, time-consuming process. Jesus says that God's rule in our lives is like that sometimes. It is like a tiny mustard seed that seems like a throwaway, until it sprouts and grows. It is like yeast, that seems like useless powder until you see what it does to a lump of bread dough.

Sure, we think, I can surrender to God. But what difference will that really make? The subtle, seemingly negligible rule of God sets all other powers on their heels. It destroys the hobbles that bind us. This does not always happen in a flash of freedom, but often in a long, challenging season of reflection, growth and change. It allows us, like a running horse, to bring our strength and grace into God's service.

Questions to think about:
1. Have you ever ridden a galloping horse? If so, what was that like for you?
2. What would it be like to endure a disability for eighteen years?
3. What are your hobbles, if you can identify them?
4. What would it look like this week for God to set you free from one or more of those hobbles?

Luke 13:21-35

Human beings are by nature deeply self-centered. I think this is very close to what the Bible means by saying we are born sinful. It's not that we are born as axe murderers, but that we are born *selfish*. People say, "How can you look at a beautiful, innocent baby and say we're born sinful?" But a baby is the most selfish creature in the world. A baby has no sense of where it stops and others start, and everyone and everything exists simply to meet the baby's wants and needs. That's almost the definition of selfish.

We read the Bible selfishly. We read a passage and the first question we usually ask—even responsible, Christ centered followers of Jesus—is, "How does this apply to me?" That's a self-focused way of reading the Bible, and it gets us into trouble.

So in this particular passage, we more often than not read these verses and we think Jesus is talking about the end of the world, or at the very least about how I can get to heaven. "What does it mean for me to enter through the narrow door?" Well, that means that I have to be a genuine follower of Jesus to get to heaven, and not just go along with the world's wide ways. Right?

Why don't we read instead with the goal of understanding what Jesus originally meant? What situations was he speaking to, and who heard him? How did his disciples originally understand his words, and why did Luke, in this case, choose to record them? Why were these words important to Luke? This kind of reading is harder, because we have to get outside our own point of view and become students of the history and context of the Bible.

How does this contextual study help us understand a passage like this one? To start with, it's no accident that verses 31-35 are included on the heels of verses 21-30, though we usually separate them. Jesus is approaching Jerusalem, and he has a deep sense of the impending danger facing this beloved city. Jesus connects this impending danger to the Jews' rejection of God's prophets throughout history, and now specifically to their rejection of him as Messiah. So many of Jesus' parables and teachings focus on exactly this topic. (See for one example Matthew 21:33-41.) Jesus sees a kind of Jewish nationalism that idealized the Maccabean revolt a century and a half before. The Jews in that day reread the prophet Daniel breathlessly because they believed it foretold a Messiah arriving any day now (just a little irony there).

They hated the Romans along with Herod and the Jewish high priests who collaborated with Rome. In context, Jesus seems to be saying, If you allow yourself to continue thinking like this, you will be destroyed. That spirit of rebellious nationalism is the wide road that everyone around you assumes is correct. I have come to show you a different way.

In fact, that tide of nationalism *did* erupt in a rebellion against Rome in 66 AD, and Rome responded with an iron fist. After a terrible siege, Jerusalem was indeed destroyed. Jesus' followers, however, saw what was coming and withdrew to the town of Pella in Syria (as well as other places). They were able to separate themselves from this conflict because they remembered Jesus' teachings. He called them away from that kind of nationalistic fervor and armed conflict.

So is it possible that Jesus' immediate context in speaking these words, and Luke's in recording them, is looking ahead a few decades to the sack of Jerusalem and the destruction of the temple? Scholars debate at length whether Luke's gospel was written before or after 70 AD when the temple was destroyed, and that really doesn't matter a lot. Anyone with eyes to see in the decades leading up to the Jewish War of 66-70 AD could tell what was going to happen. Is Jesus also, in this context, warning the Jews that the movement he starts will move beyond a strictly Jewish one and become open to people of all different tribes and nations? That seems to be the thrust of verses 28-30. Jesus says openly that the Jews will be disgraced. The Old Testament is full of this kind of disgrace, most notably in 586 BC when Nebuchadnezzar sacked Jerusalem. Jesus also says that other nations will be welcomed into the kingdom of God in the place of the disgraced Jews who were focused on their own identity. These ideas would have been horrifying to the Jews of Jesus' day. Such a fate would indeed have been grounds for weeping and gnashing of teeth. We don't need to leap to medieval visions of Dante's *Inferno* to interpret Jesus' words.

What then, to do with the secondary question of how to apply these words to ourselves? If you can't see that an unbridled nationalism is dangerous, you haven't been paying attention to the news. Can you see how Jesus offers a different, narrower door than the triumphalism of "we're claiming this nation back for God"? Yet so many who claim to speak in Jesus' name trumpet this triumphalism. Perhaps we need to reread the Bible, starting with the gospels.

It is hard work to read the Bible this way, but it is a more honest way of coming at the text. All it really is, is good listening: Understand the speaker and what they mean, get the message clear in that context, and only then interpret it for your own situation. Good communicators do this every day. We need to learn to do this as we read Jesus' words as well.

Questions to think about:
1. Do you think you're a good communicator? Why / why not?

2. How does it feel to interpret Jesus' words in this passage in the historical context described here?
3. Why was it so hard for the Jews in Jesus' day to imagine other nations being welcomed by God?
4. What is it like for you to try to read the Bible by first trying to understand its meaning in context?

Luke 14:1-24

These verses seem to fall into three distinct units.
1. Jesus heals a man on the Sabbath;
2. He tells a parable in response to those who seat themselves in honor at a feast, and
3. He goes on to tell another parable about a banquet.

All three of these, however, are united by one basic idea. Jesus is saying there is a stark contrast between living under God's rule, on the one hand, and living according to our own desires for advancement on the other. Jesus calls out the authorities who justify preserving their own property on the Sabbath. But these same leaders say it's wrong to heal a man afflicted with dropsy (an abnormal buildup of fluids in the body, what more commonly today would be called "edema"). Jesus graciously heals the man and ironically confronts his critics with the idea that this man is at least as valuable as an ox. Point for Jesus.

Then he calls out the social grasping of his audience, those who (like we have all done at one time or another) seek to advance themselves in social situations. Have you ever wanted to be that special friend, guest, etc.? Jesus' hearers position themselves to be "honored" in this way. We all play this game. It really comes back to measuring ourselves according to what others think of us. Jesus says in effect (as he will demonstrate vividly to his disciples in a few short days, see the beginning of John 13) that if you know who you are in God's love, you don't have to worry about your social standing. If you are the beloved son or daughter of God, what does it matter whether you sit at the head table or back in the kitchen? It doesn't. Yet so often we posture and worry about where we stand with people, buying into the shame-based systems that kept the dropsy-afflicted man from being healed on the Sabbath.

Jesus is redefining the power and application of God's love. He goes on to state this theme even more radically in the third part of this section. His host has gained some basic idea of Jesus' "kingdom of God" and remarks how glorious it will be. Jesus contradicts him, saying instead: The kingdom of God is already in evidence around you. Do you have eyes to see? Here I am, the promised Messiah. And yet time after time people are rejecting me, rejecting my rule. Time after time people choose to live according to the systems and values of their shame-based human rules rather than knowing who they are as beloved sons and daughters of God. Like the seeds choked out in the soil that was crowded with thorns, the characters in the parable fill their lives with concerns that are all about them and their own advancement rather than about Jesus' authority and kingship. So, Jesus says, the master of the banquet—in this case himself—will turn away from those who reject him. He will pour out his welcome on those who seem completely undeserving. Jesus is looking ahead to the scandalous invitation into God's love that will be expressed through the lives of his followers from his resurrection until the present.

And yet so often, we who *should* know Jesus' love and authority best create systems and hierarchies that protect ourselves. We build walls to keep out those we don't like. Over and over again we see Jesus turning away from those who build their own kingdoms. He turns toward those who are pleased to know themselves as beloved sons and daughters of a gracious God. They know themselves this way not because they've met some standard, but because of who God is and how he has welcomed them.

Questions to think about:
1. What is the strangest thing you've ever experienced at a dinner party?
2. What are some specific ways religious people often strive to make themselves look good?
3. What is your reaction to Jesus' parable of the wedding feast?
4. Do you think the church today reflects the master's outlandish invitation in the parable? Explain.

Luke 14:25-35

One of the silliest and most pervasive mistakes Christians make is that we take good secondary things and make them our first priorities. We take our platforms and priorities to the extreme and find ourselves opposing Jesus' agenda. Nowhere is this more true than in the whole area of "family values." Because we have decided that family values is integral to Christianity, we don't know how to read this passage where Jesus seems to say negative things about family relationships.

Family relationships are critically valuable, make no mistake. The Bible is absolutely clear about this. Marriage, parenting, honoring one's parents and grandparents in word and action—all of this is tremendously important. But it is not the core of Jesus' message, nor is it the gospel. As with any secondary priority, when these things are placed in first place, they become destructive idols that actually draw us away from Jesus.

Jesus' uncompromising agenda is that through him, people should know God. In order for that to be true, we need to recognize his sovereignty. That includes his sovereignty over parents, children, spouses, etc. If you find yourself starting to object and say "Jesus would never demand anything that would draw me away from family," be cautious. You are well on your way to idolatry.

I'm not saying you should leave your family. But if you hesitate on reading Jesus' words here, take that to him and talk it out. Would your parents, spouse, children, coworkers, boss—would they say Jesus is your first priority, over and above your dedication to them? Can you say unequivocally that he is Lord and they are not?

Jesus knows that following him is costly. He gives several disturbing examples near the end of this chapter to show that not all of us will choose the economics of his lordship. Count the cost, he says. If you can't make the commitment, recognize that. Own it. Be realistic about it.

When marriages or parenting relationships are fully in line with Jesus' lordship, they are a tremendous blessing. In God's plan, for example, marriages should be joy-filled partnerships. Christ-centered marriages glorify him, build signposts of his kingdom, and model for the world what the love of God looks like in all its exuberant joy. They are bastions of tender forgiveness and passionate partnership. They reflect Jesus into this world. Even our marital conflicts ought to point back to the love of God, in his plan. There's lots more we could say about this. But when we assume that a marriage is a Good Thing and therefore we should sacrifice everything for it, even our connection with God and our sense of his leading, we have created a golden calf for our own worship. We do the same thing (so much) with children and with parents. Read the gospels, and you'll see that Jesus confronted people about each of these relationships. Jesus demands to be Lord, in every way, over every relationship.

Dietrich Bonhoeffer, near the beginning of his final book *Ethics*, said that God's intention in the Garden of Eden was that we would know only him. Knowing God in this way, we would receive all other things *through* him. The problem of sin was that we chose to know good and evil apart from knowing God. One of the implications of this idea, that we know only God and all other things and relationships through God, is that Jesus becomes the intermediary. He mediates between parents and children, between husband and wife. We don't have immediate relationships with anyone or anything, but we receive each relationship and each experience *through Jesus*.

This is what the hyperbolic language of "hating" father and mother, spouse and children, means in Luke 14. Jesus is not calling us to despise those people, but he will not be compromised in his lordship.

Questions to think about:

1. Describe your family of origin. What is / was best about it? What is / was most difficult?
2. Can you think of good things that should be secondary, but we make them idols? Explain.
3. How do you react to Jesus' demand that he must be Lord even over our family relationships?
4. Reread the idea from Bonhoeffer's *Ethics*. What is your reaction to this idea?

Luke 15:1-10

We're splitting this chapter up unfairly, as the three stories go together as a unit. Like any good joke about a lawyer, a doctor, and a minister, the punch line always develops off the third facet of the story. Jesus makes his main point in the story of the two sons after setting things up in the first two parables.

So what does Jesus set up in these ten verses, in stories of a lost sheep and a lost coin? The stories focus, of course, on the searching and the searcher and especially on the heart of the searcher. We may often miss Jesus' groundwork here: The shepherd lays the sheep on his shoulders "rejoicing." He calls his friends together and enjoins them to "Rejoice with me." And Jesus emphasizes that there is "joy in heaven." Similarly, the woman who finds her coin after a diligent search calls her friends and neighbors together and says, "Rejoice with me." And Jesus repeats that there is "joy in heaven" over a sinner who repents.

Can we miss the fact that God is joyful, and that his friends rejoice with him? Remember the context. Jesus is telling these stories while he's hanging out with sinners, and the religious leadership is looking down their noses at the proceedings. Even before Jesus gets to his main point in the third example, it's clear that he's saying these religious leaders are not reflecting the character of a rejoicing God. Their condemnation of these sinners means that they have mistaken the heart of God, or that they simply don't care about it. Their own standards of piety and performance exclude these sinful people, and that's what matters. There is no joy in their carefully structured moralism.

Do you know the joyful heart of God? We so often bring baggage of our own. We bring performance anxiety, perfectionism, wounds from overbearing parents, discouragement from unrealistic standards we apply to ourselves. Then we project these things on to God, so we feel unacceptable. But this is not the heart of God. God is not looking at you and wishing you'd get your act together. If you are coming to him eager for fellowship, he is *joyful*. He *rejoices*. This is a God who throws a party when you come close to him!

We have to check ourselves, especially those of us who have been following Jesus for a long time. We have to check ourselves to make sure we are not aligning ourselves with the judgmental religious leaders. Are we rejoicing with the sinner who repents, or are we looking out at the world with an evaluative, condemning eye?

Questions to think about:
1. What is it like to desperately search for something precious you have lost, then you find it?
2. How many times in these verses does Jesus use the words "joy" or "rejoice" or "celebrate," etc.?
3. If all you had was these two stories, what picture would you get of heaven's priorities?
4. How have you struggled with unrealistic standards? Why is it so easy to project these onto God?

Luke 15:11-32

This story–the third in the series Jesus tells to make the same point in greater depth–has rightfully been the subject of countless sermons, devotions, books, and conversations. As just one example out of the multitude, I recommend Henri Nouwen's *Return of the Prodigal* as an excellent way into the story. The book is a slightly cleaned up version of a deeply difficult season in Nouwen's life when he felt himself alienated, cut off. He was much like the younger son in the story after the famine struck. It's a meditation on what it means to return to the Father and find yourself loved and welcomed. Nouwen later published his own more personal reflections on that season in the book *The Inner Voice of Love*. Both books are well worth your time, especially if you find yourself in a season of brokenness, repentance, or perhaps frustrated hope. In those times, we need to connect to the heart of a heavenly Father who seems absent but who, in reality, absolutely loves us.

That is the core of Jesus' story. As we said about the earlier stories of the lost sheep and the lost coin, the stories focus on the heart of the Father for those who are lost. This third story of the lost sons is told with subtlety and craft, showing Jesus at the pinnacle of his ability to communicate his Father's love through his words. Every detail of this story is worthy of reflection, and the deeper you dig the more you discover.

Evangelical Christians have traditionally focused on the younger son because he fits the theological framework of evangelicalism so well. He has strayed, his sin catches up with him, he repents and returns to the Father and is welcomed into the household. It's a great story and countless conversion testimonies over the years echo its themes. As great as it is, this is only part of Jesus' teaching here, because the literary structure of the story focuses on the older brother.

If we ask what Jesus' point was in telling this story, we cannot escape the conclusion that he focused the story on the older brother. The story ends very specifically without resolving the question: What will the older brother choose? In context, you can see why Jesus would tell it this way. The tax collectors and sinners have already welcomed him and recognize him for who he is: Jesus is the incarnation of God's love for them. He is the Messiah who leads them to the Father. He is the King of a new kingdom ruled by God himself. They get it, both in the sense of perception and in the sense of receiving the benefits of Jesus' kingship. No, the question is what the religious leaders, the captains of moralism, will do. The end of the story leaves them standing outside the party, fuming about the unfairness of God in welcoming sinners and not rewarding good people. The father's final words in the story get at the heart of God, as we saw in the first two stories in this chapter: "It is right for us to celebrate," the father says to his older son.

But why is the older son angry? If you've ever been the older son, it's not hard to see. He has done everything right. He has sacrificed self-indulgence and walked the narrow line of good behavior. He has turned away from his own pleasures for the greater good time and again. He has kept his nose to the grindstone, and frankly he has little patience for those who are not as dedicated and self-disciplined and focused as he is.

Thing is, he is sentencing himself to live as a servant, not as a son. Read the story carefully and you'll see that the older son had received his inheritance as well, but he has failed to take up both the authority and joy of his father. The father divided his inheritance between the two sons, yet the older son accusingly says, "You never even gave me a goat so that I might celebrate with my friends." The father's response is, "Son, the goats are all yours! Throw a party and celebrate!" It might just be that the older son's problem is not with his younger brother ("this son of yours") but with parties themselves. He doesn't know joy. He can't receive celebration into his heart. What a tragedy. And yet, how many Christians live there?

Has God found a way to let his joy trespass into your life? As we grow to adulthood, there is a necessary time of learning responsibility, and this learning militates against joy in some ways. Duty is important, but it is not the only thing. God eventually needs to break us down in order to impart joy into our lives. Without joy, without that hearty-partying exuberance of God's celebratory love, the gospel becomes a grim game of "thou shalt" and "thou shalt not." Like the older son, sometimes we are called to drop dead to our rigid images of ourselves and to come in and dance.

Questions to think about:
1. Is this a familiar story to you? If so, is this a different way to interpret it?
2. Who do you identify most with in this story?
3. What evidence is there that the older son is the focus of the story?
4. Why do you think so many Christians live with a shortage of joy in their lives?

Luke 16:1-13

We go immediately from what is perhaps Jesus' most well known, most loved parable (the parable of the Prodigal Son) to one of the least known, least understood, and frankly least loved parables. This one is often called the parable of the shrewd manager. Doesn't roll off the tongue quite the same way, does it?

There is an important continuity between these parables. Notice the audience. At the beginning of Luke 15, Luke tells us that the context for the three parables of the lost sheep, the lost coin, and the lost sons is Jesus welcoming sinners and the Pharisees disapproving. At the beginning of Luke 16, Jesus turns to the disciples (though it's clear later that the Pharisees are still listening in) and begins to explain what it really means to be his follower. The setting hasn't changed; Jesus is still at the same meal, with the same crowd, as in Luke 15. So we ignore this parable in chapter 16 at our peril.

In the parable of the lost sons and the parable of the shrewd manager, Jesus is dealing with questions of stewardship and our relationship to worldly wealth. The priority, laid out in the parable of the lost sons, is that we should know the Father's heart. In Luke 15, Jesus clearly told us that the Father is joyful, eager for relationship, determined to love sinners, running to the repentant. That is the Father's heart. In that context, we see a couple possible responses to wealth management.

The first is the younger son. He foolishly squanders his wealth for pleasure. No one would defend his spending habits in the parable. Yet how many of us, in more subtle ways, spend our resources for our own satisfaction? Whether it's buying a third home for our own enjoyment, a jet-ski because we want to play, or that pumpkin-spice latte just because we feel like self-indulgence, how many of us set as our highest priority that we want to buy things to make ourselves feel good? That's the way of the younger son.

The way of the older son seems much better, at least at first glance. He has denied himself and kept his nose to the grindstone. Trouble is, his whole life is a resentful lie. He labors under the mistaken belief that he doesn't matter to the Father and he is in fact little better than a slave. His life is a grim, joyless existence. He lusts after–and denies himself–the wealth that to him is evidence of his Father's injustice. He has completely missed his Father's heart.

The shrewd manager in Luke 16 provides a third option that looks absolutely heinous at first glance. Jesus describes a despicable man without a shred of honesty who wheels and deals his way into self-protection. He cheats his master in order to provide for himself. And Jesus clearly says that his ways are the ways of the world, not the ways of the Father. Being a self-centered cheat is not the solution.

But, Jesus seems to say–and we must not miss this–there's a subpoint under option three. What Jesus lifts up in the manager's conduct is that he used worldly wealth to make friends for himself because he knew a time was coming when he'd need protection. Jesus says, learn from the manager. A time is coming when you will need eternal protection. The things of this world will fade and die. So use the worldly wealth God provides in order to make friends who can help you out in your eternal needs.

Who can help you in that way? God alone. So the moral of the story, according to Jesus, is that we should use worldly resources to make friends with God. Yes, it's a crass, self-centered way of looking at things. But we have to read this parable also in light of the heart of the Father Jesus described so well in chapter 15. Remember, again, that there were no chapter divisions in the first manuscripts. So when Jesus is speaking and when Luke is writing, the story of the lost sons flows immediately into the story of the dishonest manager.

The Father's heart makes all the difference. God's heart longs to welcome us into his home, no matter how foolish we have been or how arrogant about our own work ethic. In either case, Jesus says, the Father's heart is to welcome you into his eternal dwelling, into the party of the angels for repentant sinners. So, use your wealth, rather than squandering it or serving it, to serve the Father! Then at the end of the day the two of you along with the angels and so many other imperfect but repentant sinners can sit down, enjoy a glass of Cabernet, and talk about the day's projects.

1. Have you ever been cheated? What happened?
2. What is your reaction to the shrewd manager?
3. What would it mean for you to use your worldly wealth to make friends with God?
4. How does the Father's heart change the way we hear this parable?

Luke 16:14-18

Luke tells us here how the Pharisees reacted to Jesus' teaching. He describes them as "lovers of money." If we're right about all of chapters 15 and 16 being about how we manage what God has entrusted to us, that means they're going to react negatively to Jesus' specific teachings here.

In point of fact, how we see the heart of God matters. If we see God as a distant sovereign with high expectations, we will react accordingly. If we see God as an indulgent guy who winks at sin, we'll live like that. What the Pharisees apparently missed—for all that they had right, and they had a lot of things right—was the joyful heart of God that passionately loves sinners. If that passion for broken, hurting people is at the core of who God is (and the Bible is so clear about this) then our management of our wealth and resources has to reflect that passion.

I'm seeing in a new way these days how these verses are connected to all that has gone before. I believe Jesus is so stern with the Pharisees because by focusing on their own morality and the morality of others, they have missed the heart of God. Jesus says that he himself fulfills the Law and the Prophets. That transforms how we read them. Instead of doing what the Pharisees did and reading the Law and the Prophets as a rule book, we now read them as setting the foundation for Jesus' own appearance and the proclamation of his kingdom. The Law does not go away, Jesus is very clear. There are Christians who claim that Jesus' followers should not read the Old Testament. Simply put, they have no biblical leg to stand on. But the reading of those books is transformed. We rightly see them now through the lens of Jesus himself. Everything in the Old Covenant is preparing the way, laying the foundation, and pointing toward Jesus and his kingdom. That's Jesus' point as he lays the hearts of the Pharisees bare.

So what to do with these few words about divorce in verse 18? This seems like such a non sequitur to us. The New Testament's teachings on divorce are nearly always taken out of context, and this verse is no exception. Why would this verse be sandwiched in between four parables about stewardship and the heart of God (15:1-16:13) and the story of the rich man and Lazarus that follows? Is this simply a pebble of Jesus' teaching that didn't fit elsewhere so Luke throws it in here?

No. We tend to import Jesus' words about divorce and the Bible's words about divorce in general into our own context. We have very little understanding of what they meant in biblical times and cultures. In the context to which Jesus was speaking, women had absolutely no rights. They couldn't own property, inherit, or serve as witnesses in court. A woman whose husband divorced her had absolutely no recourse. There was, in fact, a lively debate among the Jewish teachers of Jesus' own day as to exactly how formal a divorce had to be. The school that said a man could divorce his wife "for any reason" claimed that if he was upset with her, or tired of her, or if she burned dinner some evening, all he had to do was say "I divorce you" three times, and she was out on the street. The more formal school that had a tiny little bit of sympathy for the plight of women stipulated that the man should give her a written certificate of divorce. This certificate didn't do much. It proved that she had once been legitimately married and that there was some legitimate reason to dissolve the marriage before her husband got rid of her. Neither option (certificate or not) gave the woman anything in the way of help or rights. Women were literally considered property, like cattle or land. A man could dispose of his property as he wished, as long as he observed the proprieties.

Jesus is, in fact, continuing his teaching about stewardship–about property management. He is saying in effect that marriage (as the Bible clearly teaches) is a covenant relationship that is designed by God to reflect God's relationship with us (see for example Genesis 1:26-27 and Ephesians 5:21-33). And if that is true, the Pharisees' own attitudes about what was acceptable in the arena of divorce needed to be reexamined. "I divorce you, I divorce you, I divorce you" was a disgraceful way to treat a relationship designed to mirror God's love for his creation. The "letter of the law" interpretation of both schools of Jewish teachers, Jesus says, is not a legitimate way to end a marriage. Instead, it actively puts people in the position of breaking God's covenant heart.

What do we do with this? We no longer understand women as property. As the father of two brilliant, beautiful daughters, I'm extremely thankful for this! It is important for us to understand marriage as a covenant, as a relationship designed by God to reflect his passionate love for creation. Nowhere is the sinful brokenness of creation more apparent than in the painful throes of a marriage relationship headed for divorce. Divorce is a painful reality, because sin is a painful reality. We should do all we can to create strong marriages and to strengthen those who are struggling. We must never view divorce as an easy out. At times, hopefully rarely, a marriage relationship is so broken that it needs to come to an end. It has strayed so far from mirroring God's heart that continuing the broken relationship does more harm to the image of God than good, and efforts to get it back on track are unable to fix things.

And even in our day, we understand that property management is a huge issue in these situations. I've known too many couples who've moved in, bought a house together, etc. because they were "in love." They never bothered to get married. It seemed old fashioned, I suppose, or unromantic. But if that relationship goes bad, they start to see the legal issues involved. Dissolving home ownership, etc., becomes a painful process without legal protections. Dissolving a marriage rightly involves so much more than just moving out. Breaking a marriage—or any kind of covenant—should be hard, and heartbreaking. The legal structure of divorce, as rough as it is, provides (or should) some measure of protection for each party.

In all of this we want to know the heart of God, and experience both his grace and his conviction in their depth. Marriage and divorce are enormous issues for today's church, as they have been throughout the centuries. I've had so many conversations with people who struggle with their own broken relationships. Some of those struggles include ways the church shames people for their brokenness, wagging a moralistic finger at those who are in the middle of devastation and hurt.

But let's bring the conversation back to scripture here and see this particular verse in its context, where Jesus speaks it. Here, it's a stewardship issue. And stewardship is also a huge, huge issue for the church today. In his own context, Jesus is confronting a culture in which divorce was easy and painless for men. Women, on the other hand, had no rights and lived at risk of offending their husbands. It was unjust, wrong on so many levels. Jesus rightly confronts it as part of his teaching on how we manage our lives and all the good gifts God has given us. He doesn't give us easy answers, but (again) he points us back to the heart of God and what it means to live in covenant with him. That's the center of the next story he tells as well.

Questions to think about:
1. Are you more about rule-following or about empathy? What has made you that way?
2. Have you experienced a church dealing graciously with those who are divorced? What was that like?

3. How are marriage and divorce related to property management and stewardship in our day?

4. How does a vibrant marriage reflect the character of God?

Luke 16:19-31

Three things to say about this parable, which closes out this section (chapters 15-16) of parables we've said are focused on stewardship. Jesus clearly teaches us that we must know the heart of the Father, then we can figure out how to appropriately manage our worldly goods in light of who God is.

1. This parable is often cited as some kind of evidence of what the afterlife is like. I've heard in-depth teachings using this parable to explain that when we die, we are taken to a sort of holding area. Those who are good, God-pleasing, righteous, saved will go to a pleasant place called "Abraham's bosom" and those who are bad, condemned, unrighteous, unsaved will go to a place of temporary torment called "Hades" or something similar. Please understand that mapping out the afterlife is NOT Jesus' point here. Reading this parable that way would be a little like reading Moby Dick as a whaling manual or watching Jeremiah Johnson to figure out how to be a good trapper. Yes, that element is in the story, but it's not even close to the main point. The Bible is frustratingly, intentionally fuzzy about questions of exactly what happens in the afterlife. Many cultures surrounding Israel had extensive writings on this topic. The Egyptian "Book of the Dead" is the best

example. So one has to believe this omission in the Bible is intentional. Think about it a bit, and you'll see that it must very well be so. God doesn't want you to trust some road map of where you're headed after you die. He wants you to trust him, in this life and the next. Biblically, we are well advised to be like Peggy who, a couple days before she died, told me, "I figure all I have to do is die, and Jesus will take care of the rest." Sound wisdom.

2. Having laid the foundation of revealing the Father's heart in chapter 15, Jesus is now making explicit his advice in the first part of 16: We are to use our worldly goods to please God. The rich man (interestingly unnamed, though tradition sometimes names him Dives) uses his abundant wealth to indulge himself. He completely ignores the beggar at his gate. The first point of the story is that this self-indulgence is clearly against God's desire. Eventually the rich man will experience the consequence of his selfishness. We are not called to be like the younger son in chapter 15, squandering our resources on our own lusts. Nor are we to be like the elder son, selfishly hoarding those resources and never allowing ourselves to live like we are heirs of the estate. Instead, we are to manage our goods as a reflection of the Father's heart. The Father cares for the outcasts, the sick, the marginalized, the orphan, the widow, the slave, the prisoner, the blind, and the lame. The problem with the rich man is that his selfishness puts him directly in opposition to the Father's heart.

3. The end of the parable is one of those intriguing statements that must have puzzled people when Jesus first

uttered it but came to be extremely important in the early church. As the first Christians after Pentecost tried to tell their fellow Jews about Jesus and his resurrection, they faced tremendous frustration and disappointment. Throughout the New Testament we hear echoes of that frustration. The early church, almost entirely Jewish to start with, longed for the Jewish people to recognize Jesus as their Messiah. Here Jesus foretells that frustration, saying that even if someone rises from the dead (as he will shortly do) those who are entrenched in their own structures of religious power and certainty (the old wineskins he has talked about before) will refuse to believe him. We live with the same frustration today. Those who have a little bit of religion are often the hardest to reach with the amazing good news of Jesus.

So don't let's make this a parable about the structure of the afterlife and miss Jesus' point. In regard to questions about what happens after death, maybe we are wisest to cling to Deuteronomy 29:29, where Moses tells the people that the hidden things belong to God, but the things that are revealed belong to us and our children forever. Jesus' reveals the heart of the Father that will not even be stopped in the face of death. Nowhere is this revelation more clear than in Jesus' resurrection. We cling to that.

Questions to think about:
1. Do you wonder about exactly what happens to us after we die? Why / why not?
2. How satisfying is it to you when you read about the reversal in fortunes of the rich man and Lazarus?

3. How do you think the disciples felt when their fellow Jews would not recognize Jesus as Messiah?
4. How is this parable a good example of old wineskins that can't handle Jesus' new wine?

Luke 17:1-10

The kingdom of God Jesus came to proclaim is an upside-down kingdom. Power doesn't work according to our assumptions here. Neither does control. It is a kingdom built on God's ways, not our ways. As Jesus has revealed his Father's heart in chapter 15 and called us to the task of managing our resources well in light of the Father's character, so now he begins to apply this upside-down kingdom to our interpersonal relationships.

Don't lose the context here. Jesus is still in tremendous tension with the Jewish leaders who by and large have condemned him. Yet we know that some of those same Jewish leaders became his followers. John's gospel tells us specifically that Joseph of Arimathea and Nicodemus worked their way around to becoming disciples of Jesus. Have you ever had to forgive someone who at one point stood with your enemies? Have you had to release the wrongs done to you? Jesus recognizes both the seriousness of causing someone else to stumble (sin is no joke) and also the absolute imperative of forgiveness in God's kingdom.

Forgiveness is not a blanket statement or a universal principle. It is *excruciating*: literally, from the cross.

Forgiveness is the painful work of releasing the one who has hurt you. How hard it is not to say "It's okay" but to release the one whose sin is real, the one whose fault is so obvious to you.

At times I've heard of people who have been so angry at me that they say I am beyond forgiveness. I'm not surprised. I've also had people who have said and done things that have damaged me beyond what I can even calculate. On both sides of that coin, Jesus stands in between, mediating broken relationships, calling all sides to drop the hatchet and do the hard work of forgiveness.

Understand, we are not yet talking about reconciliation. That is a further step. Sometimes it's possible and sometimes it's not. But forgiveness is not an option, not if we want to be healthy. We will not do ourselves or anyone else any good if we say "I will hold on to this hurt, nurse this grudge, maintain this condemnation." As the wag has said, that's like drinking poison and hoping the other person dies.

Jesus calls us not to step into a position of authority that doesn't belong to us. We all love to be judge and jury. It's a human instinct, a reflex. It feels like justice at first, but it only leads to bitterness. When you've been hurt, the kingdom-of-God practice is to release the hurt to the Father. Let him have it rather than hanging onto it yourself. The New Testament is absolutely full of this, beginning with Jesus on the cross saying "Father, forgive them ..."

The heart of this surrender (and it is a surrender) is recognizing our role. We are servants in this kingdom, not judges. We are waiters and waitresses, not executioners. Humility, in other words, is not an option in this kingdom.

How can you become humble? Only, only by getting your focus off yourself. Turn your eyes upon Jesus, as the song says. Let go of the hurts. Let go of the shame. Let go of the desire for vengeance. Let go of the will to control. Focus on his face. Focus on his words. Focus on his grace. Focus on his nail-scarred hands. Take up the servant's task he has set before you and do it with all your will. Lose yourself in it. Let go of the other person's offense and seek God's mercy for your own woundedness.

Questions to think about:
1. What is the most humble job you've ever had?
2. What is your experience with being forgiven? With extending forgiveness to others?
3. How is forgiveness different from saying, "That's okay"?
4. What do you think it means that Jesus' kingdom turns our values upside-down?

Luke 17:11-19

This text is often used for Thanksgiving worship services, focusing on the one man (a Samaritan) who returns to give thanks to Jesus for his healing. A couple reflections on this fairly straightforward story:

First, it is interesting that a debilitating disease breaks down the social mores that keep Jews from associating with Samaritans. The nine Jews were apparently content having this Samaritan with them, and vice versa. Yet we know (see John 4, for example) that Jews and Samaritans didn't associate. We see this in our time as well. Terrible tragedies can bring people together and create bonds of commonality and understanding that would be impossible without a crisis.

Second, our status as "insiders" may well keep us from Jesus. Though these nine Jews are lepers and therefore outcasts, they still in some measure live in bondage to the expectations of their tradition. So when Jesus tells them to go show themselves to the priests, that hierarchy and authority structure takes immediate priority in their lives. The Samaritan, on the other hand, is far enough from the temple structures and systems that he recognizes that it is important for him to return to thank Jesus. The Samaritans had their own temple, their own priesthood, their own laws that required the same kind of obedience. This man, however, is already living as an outsider to his own cultural systems by associating with these Jews. Perhaps that gave him enough perspective to recognize Jesus more fully.

Third, the nine are simply being obedient to Jesus' words, but they fail to recognize the priority of a grateful relationship with Jesus. Once they were healed, it would have been entirely appropriate for them—as it was for the Samaritan—to return and thank Jesus before then proceeding to fulfill the law by showing themselves to the priests. It's about love and gratitude. A case study in similar contrasts happens in John's gospel. John carefully lays out a subtle comparison between the cripple who is healed in John 5, who ungratefully goes on to rat out Jesus to the authorities, and the blind man who is healed in John 9 and then stands up to the authorities as a witness to the authority and goodness of Jesus. Gratitude matters.

Fourth, Jesus seems to affirm the Samaritan in his disobedience. But a theme throughout the New Testament (and indeed, reading carefully, through the Old Testament as well) is that Jesus becomes the new temple and the new priesthood. He is both the locus where we meet God and the intermediary for that meeting. This is the theme of Stephen's sermon in Acts 7 that ends with him being stoned by the Jewish authorities. They desperately wanted to protect the temple and their hierarchy. So when the Samaritan returns to Jesus and recognizes in him the goodness and presence of God, Jesus releases him from the need to go to the temple and to the priests. This is the essence of Jesus statement that "your faith"–in other words, your relationship of trust with God through Jesus–"has made you well."

So what about us? Do we remain encumbered in the structures and assumptions of old power systems and miss what God is doing in and around us? Do we use Jesus for our own ends, but remain in bondage to our old wineskins? Often we fear the newness that truly surrendering to Jesus might mean. We fear the breakage of those old wineskins. For example, look around: In many traditionally bound churches today, God begins to simply allow the consequences of our own bondage to have sway. Those who maintain those old-wineskin loyalties are gripped by resentment, fear and bitterness. It's true in our personal lives as well. We cling to our old habits when they are clearly not working for us anymore. We are afraid of anything new, and the pain of change is greater than the pain of dysfunctional habits.

Questions to think about:
1. Have you ever seen a crisis break down divisions between people? What was that like?
2. What is your experience with expressing gratitude? Is that easy or hard for you?
3. How is Jesus the new temple? What does it mean to meet God in Jesus?
4. What old wineskins keep you from falling gratefully at Jesus' feet? How can you deal with them?

Luke 17:20-37

This is another section of the Bible that we tend to read in a very self-centered fashion. I can't tell you how many sermons and studies and teachings I've heard about this, inspiring an adrenaline rush of "Jesus is coming back at any moment, and he'll take one person out of bed and leave their roommate!" It's led to songs like Larry Norman's "I Wish We'd All Been Ready" (very catchy) and some frankly abusive teaching that has inspired terror in order to motivate people to true conversion. It's the classic "If you died tonight ..." question that is provocative to think about. But notice—and this is critically important—that Jesus doesn't ever inspire conversions based on that kind of tactic.

So what's Jesus getting at in this section? Let's make a few observations.

First, remember that "the kingdom of God" is not about some future heaven, but rather it is about the present day rule of God in the lives of believers, looking ahead to a future fulfillment. It's about God's kingship. So verses 20-21 are extremely important. There's an intentional linguistic pun in the text based on the fact that the second person singular and plural are identical in Greek. In other words, Jesus is saying both "the kingdom of God is inside you" (singular) AND "the kingdom of God is among you all" (plural). There is an internal, individual spiritual dimension to God's rule. There is also a relational, corporate reality to God's rule. Both are key parts of the kingship of God in our lives.

Then Jesus begins to teach his disciples some difficult things about what life will be like in their future. (Remember we have to try to discern what these words meant to their original hearers before we import them wholesale into our lives.) Jesus and the disciples are traveling toward Jerusalem. At this stage, they are likely on the east side of the Jordan River, traveling the road that followed the floodplain southward from Galilee. They have crossed to the east side of the river from their home territory and are traveling southward. They'll re-cross the river near Jericho, as we see in 18:35, and begin the long climb up into the hills where Jerusalem is located.

Interestingly, this puts Jesus and his followers geographically not far from the place where Lot escaped the destruction of Sodom and Gomorrah. That may be what prompted the conversation Luke records here. Remember, though, that Jesus is looking ahead to two cataclysmic events. First is his own crucifixion, coming up in a few short weeks. Second is that a generation from now, the city of Jerusalem will be destroyed by the Roman armies. These legions will surround it, lay siege to it, and eventually burn the city and the temple. These two events are beyond-comprehension devastating for Jesus' immediate audience. Jesus (like Zechariah or Isaiah or other Old Testament prophets) uses figurative language to communicate how devastating these events will be. First the crucifixion will devastate his followers, throwing their movement into absolute chaos. Then when he is raised, that event will transform this movement into something none of them could imagine right now. A generation later, as the news of Jesus' resurrection is spreading outward from Jerusalem into the whole Roman world and beyond, the Jews will rise up in revolt against the Romans and suffer the terrible consequences. Vespasian and his son Titus come with the legions to destroy anyone who would proclaim their independence from Caesar. It's not surprising that Jesus would end this section by saying, in answer to his disciples' question, "Where the corpse is, there the vultures will gather." It's tempting to consider whether Jesus might have been referring to the eagle that was the emblem of the Roman legions. In any case, his own soon-to-be-crucified body and the corpse of burned Jerusalem are both pre-figured in this cryptic statement.

Is it realistic to think that Jesus' words here are intended to be more figurative than literal? Think about the way we use language. A decisive political victory is a "landslide." A mass of refugees is a "flood." When public sympathies are changing we say "the tide is turning." An individual or a set of circumstances that seems a bit chaotic and high-energy is a "whirlwind." We do this all the time and think nothing of it. Jesus is doing much the same thing. He uses common apocalyptic expressions (familiar from the Old Testament prophets) here to help his people understand a bit of what's coming, and to prepare them for the challenging days ahead.

What do we do about applying these things to ourselves? It's certainly not a bad thing to hear these texts as warnings to be ready for whatever cataclysms might come. Jesus has spoken that message over and over again already, especially in chapter 13 where he tells his followers to live in an attitude of repentance. Make peace with God and tend to your human relationships. Be ready. Don't get embroiled in the concerns of daily life and miss the fragile nature of this existence. Watch for what God is doing and be ready to change your plans when God calls you to something new. All of that is true. AND Jesus clearly warns us not to try to calculate times and seasons when he might return.

Questions to think about:
1. How do you feel when you think about Jesus' return and the end of the world? Why?
2. What does it mean that the kingdom of God is both within (singular) and among (plural) you?
3. Does it make sense to you that Jesus might be using figurative language here? Why / why not?
4. How can believers be rightly prepared today for Jesus to return?

Luke 18:1-8

Though we often tend to be idealists when it comes to the Christian life, Jesus is not. We want to say, "God will take care of you" or "It will all come out right in the end" or "Everything happens for a reason." While those statements may be theologically correct, the life of faith doesn't always feel like the Right Answers. It gets messy.

Jesus is a realist. He understands what life is really like for those who live in a sin-broken world. He knows we need to trust daily that God is good and that he is in control of our challenging circumstances. That's what this parable is about.

Note that Jesus is not saying that God is actually like this unjust judge. Rather, Jesus is saying that sometimes our experience feels like God is behaving this way. We may feel like we have been storming the gates of heaven in prayer and still we are stuck, frustrated, disappointed, longing. Jesus' answer? Don't quit. Don't give up. Continue to lay your needs before God. Continue to pester God with your needs. Continue to pray, partly at least because the act of praying is an implicit acknowledgement that God is in fact sovereign.

The Bible is full of examples of those who trusted God, often for unbearably long periods of time, to fulfill his promises. How long did Abraham and Sarah wait for a legitimate heir? How long did David hide in caves? How long did Moses herd sheep in the wilderness?

There are so many great examples of believers who have endured challenging circumstances that tested their faith. One of the most potent for me is Dietrich Bonhoeffer's collection, *Letters and Papers from Prison*. As Bonhoeffer was imprisoned by the Gestapo during World War Two, he waited for positive word about the plots he'd helped foment against Hitler. He waited for news about his parents and the rest of his family. He waited to have any contact with his beloved Maria, to whom he had very recently become engaged. Reading his reflections is an amazing pendulum swing between hope and despair, faith and frustration.

If you are in a place of waiting, a place of frustration, a place of longing, ponder Jesus' words here. He's saying even if you are suffering, don't give up. Trusting in God can take the shape of persistent prayer. Allow yourself to believe. In the face of the immediate evidence, trust that God is good, that he is bringing his promises to fruition for your good and his glory.

Questions to think about:
1. Are you good at waiting? Explain.
2. Why do you suppose God doesn't immediately give us the good things we ask for?
3. Have you ever felt like God is being cruel or unjust? What is that experience like?
4. How can we learn from others who have had to wait, but then experience God's faithfulness?

Luke 18:9-17

I've become convinced that having the right answers is one of the biggest obstacles to a relationship with God. Don't get me wrong, I desperately want to have the right answers, just like you do. Unresolved questions are restless things, stirring us in uncomfortable ways that don't feel pleasant or peaceful. Answers are solid, certain, complete, safe.

The Pharisee in Jesus' story has the answers. He knows what's right, and he lives by those solid rules. He's grateful to have the answers, and to have the capability of living by them. He's doing things right. He knows it. It's comforting.

The tax collector in the story, on the other hand, has no such certainty. He is inadequate and needs mercy. Have you ever been in that place of needing mercy? It's a powerless, fearful, vulnerable place. Jesus affirms this man's vulnerability.

Similarly, the children in Jesus' example—and not just children, Luke tells us, but even infants—are also powerless and vulnerable. There's nothing more tragic in our minds than a child, all innocence and delight and openness and joy, that is victimized and hurt. We are rightly indignant when such horrific things happen. But Jesus says it's their very vulnerability and powerlessness that makes them an example of how we come into the kingdom of God. If we think for just a moment, we will see that this is not just sentiment, but it is absolute truth. This is the ironclad principle of the universe: If you come to God in your own capability, you cannot come under God's rule. The kingdom of God is about God's sovereignty and control, not yours. It is about your trust in a good, good Father.

Often God brings us into that place of trust and vulnerability by asking us questions. As I write this, I've been reading through 1 Kings in the mornings. This morning I read the story of Elijah after his showdown with the priests of Baal, running for his life into the wilderness trying to avoid Jezebel's murderous intentions. He came to the mountain of God and hid himself in a cave, and God asked him a question: "What are you doing here, Elijah?" Elijah gives an answer full of his own identity and certainty about his condition. Then God does an interesting thing: He reveals his power. Wind, earthquake, fire pass before the mouth of the cave, and Elijah does not engage. But when the sound of a "crushing silence" as one of my seminary professors read it, or a "low whisper" as the ESV translates it, shows up, Elijah recognizes the presence of God. God's silent whisper asks Elijah the same exact question a second time, and Elijah recites the same self-pitying answer a second time. Elijah, in his burned out state, can't see the possibility of change. In mercy, God decommissions Elijah and transitions his ministry to Elisha. "What are you doing here?" might seem like a simple question, but it reveals Elijah's heart. What questions is God asking? Seemingly simple questions can be the root of powerful opportunities. What do you really want? What's most important to you? What are the hurts you bear? What brings you joy? God loves to ask us questions that push us back just a bit into that off-balance place. There, face to face with God, we can be a little vulnerable. There the possibility of change becomes real.

If you want another example, look at the last few chapters of the book of Job. After dozens of chapters of eloquent speculation from Job's friends, God finally shows up before Job and–you guessed it–asks him questions. "Stand before me like a man," God demands, "and I will question you."

Recognizing that we have more questions than answers might be one good way to do what Jesus recommends here–to "humble ourselves." Humanly speaking, this is not our first inclination. But it is a sure entry point into the kingdom where God (not us) reigns supreme.

Questions to think about:
1. Would you rather be confident and wrong, or vulnerable and right? Explain.
2. What qualities of children is Jesus lifting up in these verses? Why do you think he does this?

3. What is one area of your life where you have been (or need to be) humbled before God?
4. What questions is God asking you lately?

Luke 18:18-30

This incident as recorded by Luke is so full of richness and subtlety that we often miss. There are layers upon layers of meaning and allusion here to be unpacked, and we won't get to all of them by any means. But let's take a stab.

Luke simply identifies the questioner as a "ruler." The Greek is *archon*. It is a generic term for anyone in power, not specifying office or authority. It's the same word Paul uses a few places. Depending on context, Paul might be referring to Roman authorities (up to and including Caesar) or spiritual powers (angels, demons and the like, especially those given authority over specific geographic regions) or several other possibilities of "powers." Combined with the Greek word *polis*, or 'city,' Luke uses this word to refer to the bureaucratic officials of Thessalonica in Acts 17. He calls them the *politarchs*. So we don't know much about the man who questions Jesus except that he has authority, power of some kind. Through the story we will learn more, but this is enough to start with.

Having power changes people. If you have been in a situation where you have power, you know that you have a sense of agency, of the ability to make decisive changes. If you have been in a place where you have no power, on the other hand, you feel like a victim. There's literally nothing you can do to influence your situation. The contrast couldn't be more stark. The fact that this man is a ruler, that he has authority and power in some measure, shapes everything that happens between him and Jesus.

"What must I do to inherit eternal life?" He doesn't ask "Who should I beg for eternal life?" or "How is eternal life given?" The question implies that he can make things happen, which is interesting. Even this powerful man frames the question as an issue of inheritance. By definition inheriting something is at least partially beyond one's control. There is a deep and rich theology in the New Testament of our inheriting eternal life through the death of Jesus. Paul is especially good at this in Romans, but here the ruler seems to think he can influence the execution of Jesus' will (puns intended).

Jesus plays along, eventually, but first he needs to call out the man's assumption: Why has the man addressed him as "Good Teacher"? The ruler uses the word *agathe* which means ethically, morally, or spiritually good. It's not just good as in "I'm having a good day" or "that was a good meal" but rather the deeper sense of "You are a *good* person" or "That was a *good* thing to do." It carries some weight. It's right up against the word "holy," and Jesus focuses on it for just a moment. Why, he asks the ruler, did you use that term to describe me? "No one is good but God alone." To the ruler this must have seemed like a rebuke in the moment. However to the disciples standing nearby (who had for some time been growing into this understanding) and to us reading later, it is obvious that the ruler has glimpsed something of Jesus' true nature. Jesus is, in fact, the God who is good. Goodness, uprightness, righteousness are his essence.

Before we can spiral down the rabbit hole into that topic, however, Jesus moves right along. He says, in effect, you already know the answer. Here is a basic recitation of the Law. What Jesus does not say here is critically important. He cites five of the Ten Commandments, and every one he cites comes from the later part of that list. Jesus cites the commandments that apply to relationships between humans. He doesn't cite the first few that have to do with loving God above all others. And note that Jesus doesn't say that keeping the commandments will give the man eternal life. It is extremely interesting to contrast Mark and Luke's versions of this story with Matthew's. Matthew is written to a primarily Jewish audience who understood the Law as a covenant like a marriage covenant. They saw the Torah as a relational guideline to living in love with God, rather than a rigid set of ethical expectations as the gentiles and much later the Reformers would have it. As post-Reformation gentile Christians in the 21st century, we usually read these words through those filters and have a hard time getting back to the subtleties of a Jewish understanding of the Law per Matthew's version. Luke is often a better version for us to read because, written to a gentile audience, it removes the need for at least one layer of required trans-cultural translation. Jesus here is indeed a Good Teacher, and in this case he is at least partially setting up his student by revealing what the student has implicitly understood: Though he has lived according to the rules all his adult life, he still lacks something.

Sell all that you have. Jesus speaks incisively into the man's soul, diagnosing his particular idolatry. This is not an eternal principle to be rigidly applied across the board, though so many of us are in bondage to our worldly wealth that it often seems like it. To generalize Jesus' directive here might require us to ask something like, "What owns you?" What possesses you? What is too dear to give up? What is that treasure that pins the location of your heart? We all have idolatries that keep us from leaping to follow Jesus. Do you know yours?

To put a different twist on things here, we might say the ruler is teetering on the verge of falling in love with Jesus. He is captivated by the beauty and goodness he sees in this Messiah, and he longs to have what Jesus seems to possess—eternal life. But like the young Ebenezer Scrooge confronted with the possibility of life-changing love, the ruler cannot escape the clutches of his hunger for wealth. Jesus stands before the ruler and implicitly says, "I have what you lack. Let go of what holds you back and come with me." A generation later the author of Hebrews will lay this before us explicitly (Hebrews 12:1-2). "Let us lay aside every weight and the sin which clings so close and look to Jesus, the author and perfecter of our faith." This is the choice that confronts the ruler. And sorrowing, he chooses his idolatry.

Jesus sees his sorrow and recognizes it for what it is. We sometimes speak as if freedom—political or spiritual—is simply a beautiful gift that is obviously better than any kind of bondage. However, as Ursula K. LeGuin has written:

*"Freedom is a heavy load, a great and strange
burden for the spirit to undertake. It is not
easy. It is not a gift given but a choice made,
and the choice may be a hard one. The road
goes upward toward the light; but the laden
traveler may never reach the end of it."*

In Jesus' day as in ours, people saw wealth as a mark of
God's favor. Who hasn't envied a Bill Gates? Who hasn't
wished at some point to win the lottery? Jesus explicitly
states what the wealthy learn by hard experience: Having
too much is no gift. The strings of wealth can tie us too
much to this world and its ways. Peter (v. 28) seems to be
looking to Jesus for reassurance. We've left our homes, he
says. Have we done better than this ruler? Jesus affirms
the choice Peter and the other disciples have made. Jesus
himself is the treasure. To have him, it is worth selling all
else. He is the one relationship worth having. And having
him, casting all aside to have him, we receive back again
riches beyond measure, relationships of depth and quality
that heal and enrich our hearts, family and community and
love and so much more.

Trouble is, the losses look so fearful from the ruler's side.
Death looks like a terrible ending from our perspective.
Resurrection and all that goes with it seems like a myth, a
dream. Love seems like an impossibility. But the risen
Jesus stands as witness to the reality of abundant life. The
life of eternity is not just for some far-off heaven, but
starting here and now. Let it all go for my sake, Jesus says,

and suck the marrow out of the bones of this existence.
That is the reality of following Jesus.

Questions to think about:
1. What strikes you most as you read about this rich
    young ruler?
2. Would you be more likely to say you are a powerful
    person or powerless? Explain.
3. Have you ever inherited anything? What might it
    mean to "inherit eternal life"?
4. Why might this young man have walked away
    sorrowful? Did he know what he was giving up?

Luke 18:31-43

It might seem odd to put these two sections of Luke 18
together, but this is important.

In verses 31-34, Jesus lays out a graphic description of
what is about to happen to him: betrayal, arrest, torture,
death, resurrection. We, like the disciples, are not inclined
toward the redemption of suffering. We would rather avoid
suffering and experience victory without loss or pain. In
essence, this is what it means that the disciples "did not
grasp what was said." They had come to know Jesus as
king, as Messiah. They assumed that his dogged progress
toward Jerusalem was a procession toward enthronement.
Sure, there might be battles, but Jesus would be victorious.
There might be resistance, but they were confident in
Jesus' ability to sweep away every power. Hadn't they

seen him heal the blind, cast out demons, feed the multitude? Jesus could do anything!

Our human inclination is to put our heroes up on pedestals. We prefer Superman, faster than a speeding bullet, over a crucified Messiah. The strongest evidence of our fallen human condition is that we so completely mistake the nature of love. The nature of God is to love. Love by its very nature takes the pain of the beloved into itself. This is not a codependent syndrome, but a redemptive suffering. Isaiah nailed it when he said six hundred years before, "By his stripes we are healed." Love does not march into battle victorious. It enters into pain and brings healing. Love by nature requires vulnerability. Vulnerability by definition includes the possibility of being wounded ourselves. To love is to be at risk. Without risk there is no possibility of intimacy and little possibility of relationship. We underestimate the brokenness of creation—including ourselves—and therefore mistake the nature of God's victorious love.

The cross is not an exception in the life of God; it is the nature of redemptive love, always and forever. Love as the chief character quality of God is written into the fabric of the universe, deeper than the laws of thermodynamics or gravity or 'an eye for an eye.' Sin turns us away from this truth. Sin turns us toward cheap victories that don't cost our suffering. Sin turns us away from the necessity of sitting patient with pain while it does its work. Like Inigo Montoya at the top of the Cliffs of Insanity in *The Princess Bride*, we hate waiting. So we mistakenly see suffering as the opposite of God's love, while more often than not suffering becomes the necessary groundwork for God's love to become known in a deeper way.

On the heels of Jesus' words about his impending torture and death, he encounters a blind beggar. Here is the victorious healing, the supernatural sign. But see how the beggar cries out in his desperate condition, in spite of opposition from the crowd. The people see themselves as part of a victory procession. They are enjoying a royal parade toward coronation. Little do they know what Jesus' throne will actually be and what crown he will actually wear! The last thing they want to be bothered with is the spectacle of a blind man who wants attention. In subtle and obvious ways, we shove our suffering out of sight so we don't have to deal with it. The aging go to nursing homes; the dead go to funeral homes; the sick stay home from work; we don't talk about depression in polite company; we pop pills to take the edge off our pain. When we get addicted to our painkillers we hide away in rehab centers. But Jesus stops the parade and summons the blind man. In fact he commands the people to deal with the man's blindness directly by guiding him to Jesus.

What to do with these verses? Start with sitting by the road, watching what looks to us like a victorious parade passing by. Everyone else seems to have their act together. They are successfully following a victorious Messiah en route to his coronation. There we sit in our blindness. But don't accept the illusion. This is not a victory parade, from glory into glory. We are simply watching the world parade its illusions. And when Jesus comes, realize the nature of the Love that is passing by.

Jesus goes to the cross for this deluded multitude, and for the sake of the city that will approve of his crucifixion, as well as for us. Cry out to Jesus in the place of your suffering, and don't let the crowd's misconceptions silence you. "Jesus, Son of David, have mercy on me!" He will not fail to hear your cries. He may use your suffering to confront those who simply want to march up to Jerusalem for a coronation party. He will enter into your suffering and stand with you in compassion. And he will bring healing, because he loves you. In the healing, he will invite you to enter into suffering—not just your own, but others'—and stand with a broken world in love.

Questions to think about:
1. Who was / is your favorite superhero? Why?
2. Have you ever felt like you were watching someone else's victory parade? How did that feel?
3. What is it like to picture yourself as the blind man, sitting by the side of the road?
4. Do you agree that "suffering becomes the necessary groundwork for God's love to become known"? Why / why not?

Luke 19:1-10

Frogs are low and slow, awkward and cold and clammy. Once upon a time there was a frog, the froggiest of them all, and he lived unpleasantly in his frogginess. Until, that is, the day when a beautiful princess picked him up, kissed him full on his froggy lips and ZAP! Suddenly he was a handsome prince. Not perfect, of course, and struggling to work out the details of princely existence, but transformed nonetheless.

What is the task of the church? To kiss frogs, of course.

Trouble is, most churches are built to keep frogs out. If you've ever been a frog, you know how hard it is to gain entrance to churches with their perfect-seeming people, plush carpets, careful moral codes, and general intolerance for the eating of insects. Stop being a frog, they seem to say, and we might let you come inside.

But Jesus. Jesus stops the parade through Jericho and turns to the froggiest of them all, Zacchaeus the tax collector, and says "I'm staying at your house today." At the end of the story, Jesus sums up his mission perhaps as succinctly as he ever does: The Son of Man came to seek and save what was lost.

To kiss frogs.

If we doubt this mission has been handed on to us, look at the end of John's gospel. "As the Father has sent me, so I send you." It's actually fairly simple. As Jesus was to Zacchaeus' world, so the church is to be to this world in which we live. We are to put into practice what Jesus achieved. Or, to mix in a wholly different metaphor, to play the music that Jesus wrote.

If you're still a frog, there's hope. And if in some measure you've been kissed, transformed by the caress of love into a prince or princess yourself (though I daresay you still crave the occasional housefly) your task is to love Jesus who is transforming you. And, of course, to watch with compassion for frogs who need kissing.

Questions to think about:
1. What is it like to catch and hold a frog? How is that like Jesus' interactions with Zacchaeus?
2. How is the church's mission in this world like a princess kissing frogs? How is it unlike that?
3. What is one area of your life in which you still feel like a frog? How is Jesus dealing with you in that?
4. Can you think of some frogs in your neighborhood who need kissing?

Luke 19:11-27

This parable sometimes suffers from familiarity. We think we understand it: God gives us gifts, and we are to use them well. Good enough, so far as it goes; but there is a lot of depth and backstory we miss if we make Jesus' complex story here into a simple fable with a moral.

In Jesus' world and time, the idea of a nobleman going to a far country to receive kingship was all too familiar. The various Herods for a couple generations had been seeking the favor of their Roman overlords to receive kingship, governorship, tetrarchy, or whatever other scraps Rome was willing to dispense. They had survived changes in the political winds by currying Roman favor. And they were summarily resented and even hated by their Judean subjects. Josephus tells us that when Herod the Great was dying, about the time the child Jesus was learning to walk, Herod imprisoned dozens of the most valuable and beloved men in Israel in a stadium. His orders were that at the moment of his death they should be executed. This was for the simple reason that he wanted people to grieve when he died. Fortunately the order was never carried out, but it gives insight into the relationship between Jesus' people and their government. The idea of a hated king who went to a far country to negotiate the terms of his rule would have been all too familiar to Jesus' hearers.

Luke informs us that Jesus tells this story precisely to counter the assumption that the kingdom is coming immediately. It's tempting to make the parable into an allegory, and to a certain extent this is helpful. But more often than not, we imagine Jesus returning in our time to hold us accountable for our work or lack thereof. Helpful from a motivational point of view, perhaps; but Jesus is speaking about his own "crowning," his own taking up authority that is about to happen at Jerusalem. Luke also tells us this when he mentions that they are "near Jerusalem." Jesus' hearers are assuming, still, a political victory. They anticipate a coronation that will in some form exalt them all. In spite of Jesus' previous statements, they are not anticipating the cross. But Jesus is.

An intriguing aspect to the parable is that the citizens send a delegation after the nobleman to protest his rule. Is Jesus saying that we do this to God? We don't want Jesus to rule over us, so we protest to God about the way he's running his empire. We don't want to follow a crucified, shamed Messiah. We don't want to take up our crosses and follow. "God, I just want to be victorious!" Like the third servant with his handkerchief-wrapped coin, we want to avoid risk and simply reap rewards.

Possibly the most important part of this parable is that Jesus gives us insight into how we view God, and how God honors our perceptions. The third servant launches into a detailed description of his master: "You are a severe man. You take what you did not deposit, and you reap what you did not sow." Surprisingly the master just rolls with it. "You knew, did you, that I am like that? Well, I will judge you by your own words." What is your perception of God? What do you assume about God's character, and how accurate are your assumptions? Do you assume God is disappointed in you? Waiting for you to shape up? Angry because you've failed? You will receive the judgment of these inaccurate assumptions. Our failure is not usually in doing something wrong, but in failing to know the heart of God accurately. Verse 26 gets at the heart of this. Have you noticed how some people seem to enjoy the "green pastures" of the psalm no matter what is happening in their lives? They navigate challenges and difficulties with a deep sense of being blessed and favored by God, even in the midst of hardship. This is because they have come to know God's character. They know his measureless love and tenderness for them. They know that he is in fact *for* them, that they are beloved by him.

The next few chapters of Luke's gospel will set the stage for us to know God in this way–to know his loving, self-giving heart in its fullness.

Questions to think about:
1. Has anyone ever trusted you to make investments on their behalf? What happened?
2. How might Jesus' parable here be related to the Herods going to Rome to seek kingship?
3. How might Jesus' parable be related to his own crowning as king on the cross in a few days?
4. What makes it hard for us to accept the loving, self-giving character of God?

Luke 19:28-48

What seems at first glance like three distinct episodes—Jesus' triumphal entry, his weeping over Jerusalem, and the cleansing of the temple—are in fact closely related and provide key insights into Jesus' identity and mission.

Palm Sunday sermons frequently point out the kingly symbolism in Jesus' triumphal entry, and rightly so. Rarely, however, do we take note of what Luke is at pains to point out: Jesus is returning just like the ruler in the story Jesus just told. Luke tells us that the triumphal entry happens "when he had said these things"—a clear arrow pointing back to that story. Jesus is entering Jerusalem to take up his kingship, and he will be no more welcome than the ruler in the story. His followers descending the Mount of Olives toward Jerusalem recognize what Jesus is doing. Partly at least. They get the fact that he is coming as king, and they cheer his procession onward to Jerusalem.

As Jesus comes down the hill–the same hillside where he will be arrested in a few days–he looks across the Kidron Valley to the city. It is an amazing view of the temple mount from this roadway. Jesus weeps for this city that he loves. He looks ahead forty years into the future when the Roman legions will tear Jerusalem's walls to the ground and burn its temple. He states clearly that the things that could make for peace are hidden from the eyes of his people. Thematically, it's not hard to summarize what Jesus is talking about here: repentance (see Luke 13) and recognizing him as God's chosen king are the main things required for Jesus' people to know peace. What will occur in the next few days–Jesus' rejection, betrayal, arrest, and crucifixion–fly in the face of Jesus' prescription.

Perhaps the people's rejection of Jesus is understandable, given what he does next in his presumptive authority as king: He enters the temple and cleanses it, driving out those who own the temple franchise, who change money for temple coinage and sell authorized sacrifices to worshipers. In spite of this in-your-face action, Jesus continues to teach in the temple daily, almost daring the authorities to silence him. They take their plotting underground rather than risk the displeasure of the people. The stage is set for Jesus to be betrayed and arrested. However, first we get to hear some of the exchanges that happen between him and the temple authorities during this tumultuous week.

Questions to think about:
1. If you have ever been in a church service on Palm Sunday, what was that like?

2. How do Jesus' triumphal entry into Jerusalem, his weeping over the city, and his cleansing the temple fit together?
3. What do you think of Jesus being so visible when he knew the Jewish leaders wanted to arrest him?
4. What does Jesus weeping over Jerusalem, the city where he was about to be killed, tell you about his heart?

Luke 20:1-18

The two related pieces of this text force us to examine a Jesus with sharp edges. The New Testament is clear that Jesus comes as judge. Our normal picture of what this means, of Jesus sitting on a throne saying "This one's a sheep ... this one's a goat ... sheep ... goat ... goat ... sheep" is incomplete at best. This picture probably messes us up in some significant ways. In these eighteen verses we see a clear example of how Jesus judges people. If we're paying attention, we might find out something about our own call to "judge" and what it looks like for Jesus' followers to act as judges over the world.

First section: Verses 1-8:
The Jewish leaders (who are nervous about protecting their own authority) come to Jesus to challenge him. They want to know why he sees his own teachings and actions, which are often critical of the current leadership, as legitimate. Where does his authority come from? Jesus recognizes that it's not an honest question, so he poses a question in return. He asks about the legitimacy of John's

practice of baptizing people who came to repent and thus align themselves with what God was doing. The leaders had stood at a safe distance evaluating John's movement, of course, so they couldn't answer either way, and they realize it. Recognizing their unwillingness to commit, to be judged, Jesus refuses to answer their question. And in their actions, in their unwillingness to side with Jesus even if he is legitimate, *they judge themselves.* (For a longer, but extremely provocative take on this, read C.S. Lewis' excellent book *The Great Divorce* and get multiple examples of what it looks like when people judge themselves.) They reveal the state of their unrepentant hearts. Jesus doesn't need to say, "See? You're a bunch of unholy jerks." Their self-protective unwillingness to interact honestly with the truth is visible for everyone to see.

Second section: Verses 9-18:
Jesus tells this story not to scold them, but to put their actions in context. He chooses the familiar imagery of a vineyard (see Isaiah 5, for example). This was a common way of speaking figuratively about God's chosen people. Jesus asks through this story, have you authorities been faithful tenants? Have you recognized the rights and supremacy of the owner rather than just serving yourselves? Through Jesus' story, the lesson finally starts to sink in. When Jesus tells what will happen to the tenants of the vineyard, the leaders perceive that he speaks about their future. They respond "Surely not!" If Jesus is simply telling a story, why does it matter? But Jesus is telling *their* story, making their actions clear for all to understand.

The question we have to ask, then, is this: What authority has God given you? What is the vineyard God has entrusted to you, and are you honoring him in the way you manage it?

Again, it's too easy to read this selfishly and make it all about ourselves: "Someday Jesus will come back ... maybe any day now ... and then this will be fulfilled!" Know that Jesus' words very literally came true about forty years later. The vineyard that was Israel was gutted and the current systems of leadership were completely destroyed. What wasn't completed in the Jewish War of 66-70 AD was mopped up in the Bar Kochba revolt another sixty-five years later. From that day on, Jewish leadership in the world was radically changed. Very shortly after those events, the fledgling Jesus movement became the primary voice by which most of the world could hear God's voice.

History is important, because we might be able to see in these events some parallels to our own situation. We live in one of the great shifts of the Christian movement, what some have described as a shift past "Christendom." Under Christendom, Christianity enjoyed status and privilege and power. As that power has waned, we have drifted into something we don't know how to define yet. For the moment we're just calling "post-Christendom." Is it possible that for decades and even centuries Christian churches got complacent serving themselves rather than recognizing and participating in the mission God had for them? And is it possible that in our day, God is giving that "vineyard" to Jesus-focused movements that are more true to his mission?

It's worth pondering.

In the next few verses we'll be seeing Jesus' own perspective on living in tension with culture (especially religious culture) and how to interact with a wider society that is opposed to God's rule. Hang on for the ride!

Questions to think about:
1. How do you feel as you read about the Jewish leaders' refusal to answer Jesus' question?
2. Have you ever been responsible for someone else's property? What was that like?
3. What signs do you see that we are living in a transition from Christendom to something else?
4. What is the "vineyard" God has entrusted to you these days? How is that going?

Luke 20:19-26

This brief story points out exactly how the world treats Jesus, and exactly how Jesus treats the world. Note, to start with, that the religious leaders understand (verse 18) that Jesus has publicly called them out by telling the previous parable. He has named them as unfaithful tenants in God's vineyard. Their response? They could have repented. Instead they sent spies hoping to catch Jesus in words they could later use to convict him. Note also that they have increased the stakes in the game: They're no longer just trying to smear Jesus in the court of public opinion. Their question is specifically about how to deal with the Romans. The Romans reserved the right of capital punishment for themselves. Jesus' opponents want to get him not just disgraced, but executed.

The heart of their question: Is it lawful for us to give tribute to Caesar, or not? The people hated their Roman overlords. Popular sentiment would immediately answer, who cares if it's lawful? We need to rebel! The Jewish leaders who sent these spies, however, were colluding with the Romans to maintain a relatively stable political climate so they could maintain their power base.

Jesus says it's not just a question of taxation, but of identity. Show me the Roman coin. Whose image is on the coin? (Jewish coinage, by the way, never included a human form like Roman coins did, because of the Old Testament prohibition against graven images. Luke makes very clear this is a Roman coin.) Caesar's image is on the coin, they said. So Jesus knows well that these spies as well as everyone else in earshot will get the reference he is about to make. He says they should give to Caesar the things that bear his image (i.e., the coins—pay your taxes) and to God the things that bear his image.

No listener would have missed this: In Genesis 1, God said he was going to make human beings in his own image and according to his likeness. So even in the face of this seemingly niggling question about taxation, Jesus points to the ultimate authority of God. He challenges his hearers toward repentance: You are made in the image of God. Therefore, pay your taxes to Caesar but give yourself to

God. Stop worrying about self-preservation and render your heart to God. Then see where he leads you.

It is not very hard to transpose Jesus' comments into our own era. We who tend to be so consumed with the matters of costs and benefits, of ownership and acquisition. But we must ask ourselves: whose image do we bear? And are we giving ourselves, heart and soul, to God, living as his reflections, his image, in this world?

Questions to think about:
1. How do you feel about paying taxes? Explain.
2. What do you think the Jewish leaders were hoping to get out of their questioning of Jesus? Why?
3. How do the questioners judge themselves in asking these questions?
4. What does it mean to live as one who bears God's image in this world, reflecting his character?

Luke 20:27-40

Writing and pondering this story in the run-up to Valentines Day, I suppose it's not surprising that the biggest contrast I see between Jesus and his detractors (in this case, the Sadducees) is *love*.

Ironic, isn't it, that the Sadducees' question is built around marriage. But their approach (besides the fact that they are simply using this hypothetical situation to entrap Jesus, and so love is out the window from the get-go) is legalistic. There's no pathos in their storytelling. There's no concern for the specific people in the situation. There's no compassion. It's exactly like the "lifeboat" ethics problems that were popular a generation ago: There are five people on a lifeboat, but the lifeboat can only hold two. Who will you throw overboard?

I've been reading Bob Goff's book, *Everybody Always* lately. Goff does a great job of pointing in his homespun way back to Jesus' command that we should love one another. Always. Almost without exception, our rules and principles get in the way of love rather than empowering it. We have basic expectations of human decency that are reflected in the most elementary structures of justice. Once we get beyond those, however, we fine-tune our systems to decide who is in and who is out. We draw careful lines around who measures up and who doesn't, who is worthy and who is to be discarded. There's also a serious irony here. Perhaps more than anything else, we focus these systems on ourselves and not surprisingly, find ourselves wanting. We fall short. We are broken. We have sinned and continue to sin. We don't look like the airbrushed models in the ads. We've gained a few pounds. We binge-watch Netflix. We find the most creative ways to shame ourselves. We draw circles that exclude us from being accepted, from being loved.

Without doubt, the most systematic writer in the New Testament is the Apostle Paul. He carefully reasons out the philosophical and theological underpinnings of Jesus' death and resurrection. If anyone is willing to draw hard lines, it's Paul. Yet, when he's summing up the implications of what Jesus did, Paul over and over again says it comes down to drawing bigger circles that include us all. My favorite summary of this position comes at the beginning of one of my favorite chapters in the Bible, Romans 8. Paul writes, "There is therefore now NO CONDEMNATION for those who are in Christ Jesus" (emphasis added, though it's fair to say that the entire New Testament was written in ALL CAPS in the original Greek, which is kind of funny when you think of it through the filter of today's social media conventions). No condemnation is another way of saying there's no shame. For those who are "in Christ Jesus," there's no possibility of being excluded. As Paul says at the end of that same wonderful chapter, there's nothing in all creation that can separate us from the love of God in Jesus. Nothing.

We can certainly exclude ourselves, and most of us do. We turn away from God. But the upshot of this brilliant message is that when we allow God to turn us back to himself, we find open doors and open arms. The tragedy (as C.S. Lewis so strikingly portrays in his excellent book *The Great Divorce*) is that so many of us choose separation from God. We condemn ourselves, in spite of God's superabundant love.

So the Sadducees lay a trap for Jesus, and Jesus responds with something like, "Don't you get it? It's about love, and you've completely missed the point." Human love—even the greatest human love like that in an excellent marriage—is an arrow pointing toward the real source of love, God himself and his love for us. Why would you keep the treasure map when you find the treasure? Though I suppose you might tack the treasure map up on the wall as a nostalgic reminder of the journey and what an adventure it was. In a similar way, maybe our imperfect human loves will be nostalgic reminders in heaven of God's love and how we began in imperfect, partial ways to know him and his measureless love for us.

The last point to make is this: Jesus' response to the Sadducees, though it seems harsh, was exactly what love looked like in that situation. He was confronting not their surface question, but the assumptions that kept them from knowing the living God in his fullness. The story ends on a hopeful note. Luke tells us that from that point on they no longer dared to ask Jesus any question. This is hopeful not because questioning God is wrong, but because questioning God from a position of arrogant superiority is foolhardy. One can hope that their silence came from humility and a sense of having their eyes opened to the love standing in front of them.

Questions to think about:
1. What is the greatest love you've experienced in this life, in human terms?
2. What do you think is the difference between legalism and love?
3. How might our rules oppose love rather than empowering it? When might the opposite be true?
4. What would it look like to let God's love draw "bigger circles" in your life these days?

Luke 20:41-21:4

Jesus turns the tables on his detractors. He asks them a thorny scriptural question that contradicts their common wisdom. Again, his question opens the door for them to recognize his authority if they're willing. But sadly, they are not. So Jesus speaks an open warning that his disciples, the crowds, and even the Jewish leaders can hear: Beware of them, beware of their love of appearances, of their longing for human recognition. They love status. They serve themselves rather than living in submission and dependence on God. Jesus says they "devour widows' houses." This ringing condemnation echoes many of the prophets. (Amos, for example, is lockstep with Jesus at this point.)

Then Jesus moves on to point out an actual widow. Remember that the chapter divisions were added later. If you were just reading through this text as a narrative, it would be hard to miss the obvious connection between "widows' houses" and this widow. Out of her poverty and her faith she offers her pittance to God. She becomes the poster child for trust and submission, in contrast to the scribes' scheming and self-focus. She is living out Jesus' command in the Sermon on the Mount (Matthew 5-7) to "seek first God's kingdom and his righteousness" and to lay up treasures in heaven. Jesus makes this connection explicit when he comments on her giving by saying "this poor widow has put in more than all of them."

As we'll see next time, the self-seeking power games of the scribes and authorities bring down condemnation not only on themselves, but on the temple institution and the future of Israel as a political entity. Again, Jesus echoes the prophets when he says that their agendas and refusal to recognize what God is doing will not stand.

Questions to think about:
1. Are you someone who deals well with criticism? Why / why not?
2. How does Jesus' question turn the tables on those who have questioned his authority?
3. Do you normally calculate your donations as a percentage of your income? Explain.
4. If Jesus was going to speak prophetically to our own day, what might he say to us?

Luke 21:5-38

We need to take seriously that all of Christianity is based historically, and the basis of Christianity is not our period in history, but that of Jesus.

This is so obviously important when it comes to a passage like this in Luke 21. Too often, modern readers read a passage like this purely in reference to themselves and an anticipated "second coming of Jesus." Now, the New Testament does talk about Jesus coming again, very clearly. But we so often become self-centered and read this chapter purely in reference to our own expectations.

We focus on our own anticipation of how soon Jesus might come back for us. We completely miss the point Jesus was making, and it hurts our churches. So much.

Sad to say, even deeply committed Christians rarely get to know the history of the first century. Some will know a little bit about the fact that the Jewish temple was destroyed by the Romans in 70 AD, but even that tidbit doesn't help them read their Bibles better. Instead, they go on reading as though every word was written for their self-focus.

Fact is, it is of tremendous value to read the Bible, and I believe with all my heart that God speaks to us through its words. But to read as mature followers of Jesus, we have to add a step. There is a great Peanuts comic strip that makes this point well. Linus tells Charlie Brown he feels guilty going to Vacation Bible School. They are studying the letters of Paul, and Linus agonizes that he is "reading other people's mail."

That's exactly what we are doing, and we need to take it seriously.

The original audience for Luke's gospel was a man named Theophilus, most likely a Roman official who had become a Christian. Beyond that, this gospel rapidly came to circulate within the Christian communities of the first century. They at least could read it with some sense of its proper context.

We, however, take a chapter like this one and we read it from our own perspective. We never think about the fact that Jesus' original hearers lived with a completely different frame of reference than we do. We misunderstand a lot of what Jesus said because we read in this irresponsible way.

If you doubt that Jesus intended to address first century events, you are ignoring verses 6-7 and verse 32. When we start to dig into Jesus' own context, there is a lot to learn. Where can a person start? Here are a few recommendations:

1. Get a good academic study Bible. Life Application Bibles and such are great, but if you want to dig deeper into what the Bible is really saying and learn a bit of the history, find a Bible that includes diagrams of Jerusalem, timelines of the period between the Testaments, and talks about which Roman emperors were in power when the New Testament was being written.
2. Read a few articles on an easy to understand source, even one like Wikipedia. Here are some ideas what might be most helpful to read about:
    o   The Jewish War of 66-70
    o   Several Roman emperors including Augustus, Tiberius, Caligula, Claudius, Nero, and Domitian.
    o   Study up on "apocalyptic literature" and realize what exactly it is, and what it is trying to accomplish.
3. A good historical atlas of the Bible is very helpful, whether online or in print. Often church libraries have one of these stuck back in a dusty corner somewhere.

4. Read up on Josephus, and then dabble in his histories a bit. Josephus was roughly contemporary of the Apostle Paul and wrote extensive histories of the Jewish people and a fascinating autobiography. His writings give us tremendous insights into the world of the New Testament.

How will this kind of study change your reading of the Bible? Let's start with Luke 21. What will we learn about this chapter?

- Realize the context. Jesus and his disciples are talking while they gaze at the temple, still under construction, being built out of massive limestone blocks. It was a huge project undertaken by Herod the Great. Herod died in 4 BC, but the project continued on and was finished a few years after Jesus' crucifixion and resurrection. The project was designed to intimidate and inspire. The giant white blocks (a few from the foundation platform are still visible at the Western Wall in Jerusalem, but as Jesus predicted the temple itself was knocked down completely) gleamed and gave the Jewish people a deep sense of national pride. This pride eventually led to the revolts that precipitated the Jewish War of 66-70 AD.
- Everything Jesus described in this chapter happened in the generation after his crucifixion and resurrection. But what about verses 25-33?? Surely here Jesus is talking about his own second coming? Not so fast. Don't skip over verse 32! Jesus says he is talking about the generation of his

hearers. What then, to do with the words about "the Son of Man coming on the clouds"? Here is where studying apocalyptic literature becomes helpful. While in our day we are tempted to read for some literal meaning, Jesus' contemporaries out of necessity became experts at shrouding their meanings in figurative religious language. So the book of Daniel and the book of Revelation in our Bible, along with other passages here and there, are full of apocalyptic imagery. Apocalyptic writing is designed to *hide* its meaning from the enemies of God's people but to *reveal* basic truths and encourage God's faithful people. Jesus' words here are an apocalyptic way of speaking of the rise of Jesus' own followers and the spread of his message throughout the Roman world, not of some cosmic second coming. (Though, as stated earlier, the New Testament does in fact teach about Jesus' second coming—just not right here.)

- Always, always in the New Testament when we read about these "end times" kinds of teachings, scripture points us clearly—usually in the very next breath—to pay attention to our own conduct. This passage is no exception, as Jesus brings his teaching home in verse 34-36. Watch yourselves. Stay awake. Pay attention. This is where Jesus calls us to focus. Don't get fascinated by end times speculation. Instead, do what Jesus clearly calls you to do. Meet together for worship. Pray. Steep yourself in scripture. Be kind to your neighbors.

Bear witness to all God has done for you. Don't grow weary.

Questions to think about:
1. Do you get fascinated by end-of-the-world stuff, or do you avoid it? Explain.
2. How much do you personally know about biblical history and the context in which it was written?
3. Is it disturbing for you to consider that these words might not refer to Jesus' return? Why / why not?
4. If Jesus was coming back next week, what projects would be most urgent for you to finish right now?

Luke 22:1-23

The threads of the story draw together now. The authorities have taken their stand against Jesus, and have moved from being disgruntled and upset about him to actively plotting to kill him. Jesus' disciples are nervous, even terrified, but even more they are clueless and simply trying to follow faithfully. Judas steps up to be the tool of Jesus' betrayal. He willingly puts himself in the breach between the plots of the Jewish authorities and Jesus' last few days of human freedom before his death.

What of Jesus? Do we see Jesus as a victim or victor here? In the way of biblical truth, Jesus is both. Biblical truth is usually paradoxical. We are taught to try to reconcile the extremes. But we must not choose a middle ground. The Bible calls us to live in both ends of the extremes at once. Most of the classic arguments of

Christian theology find their best solutions in this methodology. Take, for example, the ongoing debate in our day between those who say God is absolutely sovereign and all is predetermined, on one hand, and those who say we are free to choose salvation on the other. Sometimes these positions are labeled Calvinism and Arminianism, though I'm of course caricaturing both without doing justice to either. But I know prominent Christian schools that expect their students to choose one of these options. How can we do this? The only way to do Christian theology in a biblical way is to live at both extremes. Of course God's sovereignty extends to the movement of every atom in the universe. Of course God has given us mind-boggling freedom to choose. If we let go of either extreme, our theology quickly becomes twisted and unbiblical.

Jesus here is absolutely a victim. He is the innocent lamb, about to be taken by the powers. He will be forced through an illegal sham of a trial, and sacrificed via the machinations of the Roman overseers. Satan will have a field day manipulating the temple authorities, the Roman governor, the disciples, Judas, and all the rest. How can you read this story and not have a terrible, pit-of-the-stomach sense of revulsion and hopelessness in the face of such horrible injustice?

But Jesus is the victor. Like Aslan in Lewis' *The Lion, The Witch, and the Wardrobe* knowing the deeper magic of the Stone Table, Jesus deftly navigates the machinations of the world, the flesh, and the devil. He has carefully arranged allies in key positions that will allow him to fulfill the scriptures. He will tie together the threads of the

Passover into a simple meal of bread and wine that he will bequeath to his followers in the night in which he is betrayed. He directs Peter and John to the upper room like a spymaster, knowing the hours are counting down and he will soon give himself to those who will beat and crucify him. He is absolutely powerless and absolutely in control.

There is hope for us in seeing Jesus in this biblical way. We have amazing freedom to create webs of sin and error, and we deal with the consequences of our own actions. We bear our sin and its fathomless stupidity. At the same time, Jesus, the Crucified One, lives to pardon us, to wipe our slates clean. He speaks a new identity into our poisonous webs: There is therefore now no condemnation. Find yourself in me. Know yourself through my Father's words. You are my beloved, in whom I am well pleased.

Both are true. You are a sinner, deserving of complete condemnation. You are completely free, exalted in Christ to complete innocence before your heavenly Father. Jesus is inexorably headed to the cross where he will make all this possible.

You say you can't reconcile these extremes? Don't try. Hold them in tension, rather, and use each to respond to the other. When you wake up and see only ugliness in the mirror, hear the words of Jesus calling you his beloved. When you get cocky in your achievements and your holiness, be reminded that you are completely undeserving, saved only by the goodness of God's grace.

Questions to think about:
1. What is your gut level reaction to Jesus' betrayal, arrest, torture, and crucifixion?
2. How does Jesus function as both victim and victor in these events?
3. Do you usually focus more on God's sovereignty over your circumstances or on your own freedom?
4. How does it feel to see yourself at both ends of the spectrum, at the same time sinner and innocent?

Luke 22:24-38

It is the night of Jesus' betrayal and arrest. He has shared his last meal with the disciples. Now he has a few key things to teach them before he is taken from them. What will he focus on?

Jesus' initial teaching goes to the heart of his message, but it doesn't arise from a carefully prepared lesson plan. Instead, Jesus responds to his disciples' bickering. They argue about who will have the highest station in Jesus' coming kingdom. There is so much a person could say about this: the height of the disciples' rudeness, how completely they have missed his point over the past three years, the radical shift in understanding that is to come in the next few days, and more. Focus for just a moment on what seems to be Jesus' key point. He contrasts the world's understanding of authority and greatness over against his own kingdom and a kingdom-based understanding of power. Jesus says "I am among you as one who serves."

Then Jesus says something that, if we're not careful, sounds like underneath it all he truly does buy into this world's views on power. He affirms that the disciples have stayed with him in his trials (v. 28) and he goes on to say that he is giving them his kingdom, just as his Father gave it to him. He says they will eat and drink and serve as judges in that kingdom. Our initial assumption about Jesus' meaning might be that finally they will be rewarded for their faithfulness. It sounds like they will be given power like earthly soldiers being rewarded with royal positions. Be careful: Our views on what constitutes power have been so twisted by this world's assumptions. We are in great danger of completely missing Jesus here.

When Jesus assigns a kingdom to his disciples, when he affirms them for standing with him through time and trial, when he tells them they will eat and drink and judge the twelve tribes of Israel, he is not conferring titles and uniforms on them. Rather, he is telling them that as he has invited them to follow him and they have obeyed, they will step into his character and his role. He is the one who rules over the kingdom as the suffering king. He is the one who will drink the cup he is about to suffer (cf. v. 42). He is the judge who, by his very presence and by people's reactions to him, judges the nation. So the disciples will "rule" by embodying Jesus' nature as the suffering king. They will be figures of immense spiritual authority as they go out into the world to proclaim Jesus' resurrection, and they will suffer terribly. They will recognize God's plan to save the nations through Jesus' death and resurrection and through their proclamation. They will strive to be obedient to that plan. They will take up the cup of martyrdom. They will indeed inherit Jesus' kingdom. They will proclaim freedom for the captives, recovery of sight to the blind, liberty for the oppressed in the name of the risen King Jesus.

None of this confers on them the authority to raise an army, levy taxes, build a property base, or line their own pockets. When Jesus' followers have stepped into these kinds of worldly activities, we are a far cry from his kingship and his kingdom. As if to make this comically clear, Jesus advises the disciples to arm themselves (this is a tough passage for those who say Jesus is a pure pacifist). In response to Jesus' words about making sure they have swords, the disciples reply that they have two. Hardly an army! Two swords is not enough even to be an armed gang; but Jesus says it is enough.

Working through the gospel of Luke, I have been struck over and over again how completely Jesus turns the values of our world upside-down. He creates new wineskins to hold the new wine of his teaching, of himself. How hard it is for us to read his words without simply importing them into our own understandings! We must learn to know Jesus' character and read his heart. As we do, we will find ourselves bit by bit transformed until we look like him in some ways... and we will begin to take up the kingdom of servant-love he has assigned to us.

Questions to think about:
1. How are Jesus' teachings about power and authority different from what you hear each day?

2. What do you think Jesus meant when he said he was giving his disciples a kingdom?
3. How is Jesus' picture of "judgment"–that we judge ourselves by how we respond to him–different from the way we normally talk about judgment?
4. Have you been growing lately in your knowledge of Jesus' character? Explain.

Luke 22:39-62

One of the earliest Christian worship songs is recorded in Philippians 2. It talks about how the eternal Son of God did not count his status as God something to be grasped. Instead he emptied himself and became obedient to death, even death on a cross. Theologians talk about this as Jesus' *kenosis*, from the Greek word used to describe this "emptying." What we see in this passage of Luke is still more of Jesus emptying himself. At the beginning of this passage you could make the argument that Jesus is still a powerful figure. He is an influential teacher, the leader of a committed group of disciples. He has widespread appeal to masses of people and some influential friends. His miracles and his movement have drawn the attention of crowds of common people. He has been noticed by the ruling elite. Little by little, all this is stripped from Jesus.

Jesus goes in darkness to the Mount of Olives, just across the Kidron Valley from Jerusalem, to pray. This was near the home of his friends Mary and Martha and Lazarus, but Jesus stays in the ancient grove of olive trees that moonlit night. He is in agony, knowing what is to come and yearning for another way forward. His committed disciples are sleeping a short distance away. Of course they still believe themselves loyal, even to death, but they just can't stay awake.

Except Judas. Judas is wide awake. Heleads a band of thugs to this spot precisely for the purpose of betraying Jesus. The disciples try to fight. Jesus prevents the conflict from escalating. Cut off from their "fight" reflex, the disciples resort to "flight" and run off into the darkness. Jesus is left alone with his betrayer and with those who will take him to an illegal trial under cover of darkness.

Peter trails along at a distance in the dark. He longs to stand up for Jesus. But after being rebuked by Jesus for striking out with his sword (not to mention proving himself a less-than-adequate swordsman by merely cutting off a man's ear) he is uncertain. Like so many of us Peter is drawn to Jesus but afraid to take a stand.

Peter's presence provides the next step in Jesus' emptying. As long as Peter kept his mouth shut, we might believe that at the very least, scattered though they are, Jesus' followers remain loyal. We might say that Jesus still has some stalwarts hidden here and there. But Peter betrays this fantasy for what it is. Peter speaks three times, each time denying that he even knows Jesus. To make matters worse, in all likelihood Jesus hears it all..

The eternal Son of God gave up the glory of heaven. He turned from the incessant worship of angels who sang his praises and proclaimed his power. He was surrounded by immensely glorious beings whose praises rang out that it is Jesus, the Son, who holds all the universe together. He gave all that up to become human. In the measureless wisdom of God, he was born as a tiny baby in an out-of-the-way corner of Judea. We celebrate that at Christmas every year. But now the incarnation becomes complete in its unfathomable existential measure: Jesus is cut off from his community, his influence, his reputation. He no longer functions as the one who gave sight to the blind and raised Lazarus from the dead. Instead, he is now a shameful criminal, deserted by his band of rabble. He is pressed into an inquisition under cover of darkness.

He is truly what Isaiah described: despised and rejected, a man from whom we hide our faces, smitten and rejected, utterly alone, without appeal and without beauty.

Strangely, the Bible insists that Jesus did this for us. There are depths to plumb here, but for the moment let it be enough to say this: No matter what rejection you have suffered, what betrayals you have endured; no matter what loneliness haunts you, what isolation cuts you off from love and from community; no matter how your reputation has been smeared, no matter how your actions and words have been twisted, Jesus has been there before you. He has fallen deeper into the abyss than you have gone. You are not alone in the pit. The Son of God loved you and gave his life—not just his ability to breathe, not just his heartbeat, but his relationships, his reputation, his status—for you. He died the death you fear, so that you are never, can never be alone. Even if your narrative gets worse, so will Jesus' story. He has the trials, the flogging, the cross yet to endure. But in the end, he died your death. He did this so that you need not endure without hope. He rose from death so you can know you, too, will rise. He raises you not just from death but from meaninglessness, hopelessness, alienation, isolation. The Garden of Gethsemane is for you. The cross is for you. The resurrection is for you.

Questions to think about:
1. What does it feel like to be emptied, to lose relationships, status, reputation?
2. How do you suppose the disciples were feeling as they turned and fled when Jesus was arrested?
3. What does it mean that Jesus emptied himself for you? How can you respond to that love?
4. How does it feel to know that Jesus went deeper into the abyss than you could ever go?

Luke 22:63-23:16

In his excellent book, *The Day the Revolution Began*, N.T. Wright asserts that the crucifixion of Jesus initiates a revolution. The revolution, he says, is just this: *self-sacrificing love is taking over*. In fact, Wright makes a powerful argument that self-sacrificing love is the most powerful force in the universe. Jesus' life, death and resurrection start setting the broken, sin-sick universe back in line with the character of God whose nature is self-sacrificing love.

Most of us have a soft spot, however deeply hidden, for stories of "true love." While we may trivialize this term with tales of overblown heroes and heroines, there's something in us that loves a love story.

This section of Luke's gospel brings us into such a story, the most true love story of all time. But we may be surprised what love looks like. Jesus stands, in turn, before the temple guard, before the Sanhedrin, before Pilate (and Caesar, whose power is the foundation of all Pilate does), before Herod, and before Pilate again. In short, Jesus stands in apparent weakness before the greatest powers ruling over that part of the world. What power does he bring to bear in this contest?

Weakness. Jesus brings the willingness to sacrifice himself. Why? Out of love. "Greater love has no one than this," Jesus said, "that he lay down his life for his friends" (see John 15). Jesus stands without making a defense in the presence of those who have made themselves his enemies. He goes to the cross for their sake and for the sake of the world. The New Living Translation of Romans 5:10 says that "our friendship with God was restored while we were still his enemies." Jesus sacrifices himself in love for Pilate, Herod, the Jewish authorities, the temple guard with their whips and their crown of thorns, the Roman soldiers tasked with flogging him within an inch of his life, and for us.

But is it reasonable to say that Jesus' self-sacrificing love is a greater power than all these worldly authorities? Isn't that just insipid idealism?

Look at the results. The temple guard and the Roman soldiers are nameless to us. Herod is remembered by history as an egotistical tyrant in a long line of egotistical tyrants who bore that name. Pilate washed his hands to avoid guilt and is remembered for little else today but this one action. Tiberius Caesar's empire endured the ravages of history for another four hundred years before the Visigoths sacked Rome and brought the empire to a whimpering end.

In comparison, the impact and influence of Jesus has just continued to grow. This bleeding man, sacrificing himself before the authorities and powers of his day, sparked a revolution that has expanded from that day to this. The irreconcilable divide between Jews and Gentiles was bridged within a generation and continues to pull together what the world keeps trying to split apart. Jesus' followers stood loving in the face of a Greek and Roman culture that discarded the handicapped, aborted and exposed unwanted infants, and abandoned the sick. Christ-followers willingly gave up their lives to protest the grisly violence of the gladiatorial games. When Europe descended into darkness and ignorance after the fall of Rome, tight-knit communities of Jesus' followers preserved learning and invented western science. Similar communities created large-scale health care and hospitals. This movement that Jesus started became a refuge for women who were viewed as property in most cultures.

The record of Christianity has been far from perfect. Far too often those who claim the name of Jesus act more like

Herod or Pilate. But compared to what the world was without Jesus' self-sacrificing love, the changes wrought by this Galilean and his followers are staggering. Looking at the broad sweep of history, Jesus' movement has indeed been a revolution.

It is a sinking feeling to stand in the face of power, willing to be brutalized for the sake of love. But I am convinced Wright has expressed this accurately: In the long run, there is no power in the universe capable of greater things than self-sacrificing love.

Questions to think about:
1. Have you ever felt powerless in the face of power? What was that like?
2. Looking around you, would you agree that "self sacrificing love is taking over"? Explain.
3. What positive results can you think of produced by the movement Jesus initiated?
4. How does it feel to know that Jesus sacrificed himself for Pilate and Herod, and for us?

Luke 23:18-56

Looking at the crucifixion of Jesus is always overwhelming. It's a little like trying to see North America from downtown Kansas City. No matter where you look there's something significant, something that is a part of the greater whole, but it's nearly impossible to see the whole thing all at once. And like trying to see all of North America, trying to see all of the crucifixion and its implications requires getting such a distance that you really can't pick out very many details.

This moment, the crucifixion of Jesus of Nazareth under the Roman governor Pontius Pilate in about 29 or 30AD, becomes a fulcrum for the rest of time. Massive changes rooted in this moment will ripple out and transform Jewish identity and significance, the Roman Empire, and all of human history.

Why does the death of one Galilean man, sentenced to torture and death for pretensions of being a Jewish king, have such impact?

If the crucifixion was the end of Jesus' story, we would know nothing about him. We know next to nothing about so many other prophets and revolutionaries from his time period. It is the resurrection that fuels the fires and makes Jesus' impact unimaginably significant. Given that we know what comes next, we examine the details of Jesus' death and find immeasurable wealth here.

Take one tiny moment out of the narrative as an example. The story of the dialogue between Jesus and one of the two criminals crucified next to him is unique to Luke. We don't know the names of these criminals, and scholars debate if they were thieves, rebels, or what. Luke reports that one of the two recognized their sentences were just, however, and that Jesus' was not. He appeals to Jesus to "remember me when you come into your kingdom." It is an odd statement, to say the least. Jesus is hours away from death, just as he himself is. Neither will be coming down from their crosses alive. The coming hours will include unimaginable pain.

The gospels stop just short of stating the fact that the cross is, in fact, Jesus' throne, but the implication is clear. He is crowned with thorns, and the sign above his head (a Roman custom so that passersby could see the sentence for which each criminal had received this terrible punishment) proclaims him "king of the Jews." He has just completed a procession into Jerusalem in which he received accolades as "son of David." In that impromptu parade, he rode a donkey to fulfill Zechariah's prophecy of how "your king is coming to you." He has debated the meaning of his title as "son of David" with Jewish authorities. A few days earlier, when two of his closest followers asked to sit at his right and left when he was enthroned, he deflected their question. He stated that those positions were not his to grant, but that they belonged to those for whom they had been prepared. And here are the two thieves, one on Jesus' right and one on his left, as he hangs in agony and glory.

"Jesus, remember me when you come into your kingdom." Perhaps this is the plea of a dying man, looking for a way off the cross. Maybe the thief is hoping to see the miracle worker do one last amazing thing. Or maybe it's the recognition by a criminal that his sentence is just, but the universe is ruled over by a merciful God—and he is bold to ask for pardon.

Jesus' response shows that either he is privy to information unavailable to the soldiers and mockers watching him die a slow death, or else he is completely deluded: "Today you will be with me in paradise." Theologians and cosmologists have debated ad nauseam what these words mean. At the very least, they seem to provide hope for a dying criminal. Down through the ages, countless numbers of Jesus' followers have seen themselves in this thief's place, asking for mercy from Jesus in their desperate hour. Note that the request doesn't say, "Help me avoid the consequences of my actions," nor does it say "Make it as if I'd never done anything wrong." The request is simply, "Remember me." What that looks like, the petitioner leaves up to Jesus.

At the very least, such a request requires trust. Trust is perhaps the oddest of commodities coming from a man being executed on a cross. There's a lot here to learn about the nature of faith: It takes over when all other options are gone, when hope itself looks like a delusion. And in this utter helplessness, we see anew the depth and power of the incarnation of Jesus. Being in the form of God, he didn't count equality with God something to be grasped, but emptied himself. He took the form of a criminal on a Roman cross so that he could reach *this* criminal who has thrown self-justification to the wind and has simply reached out for mercy.

In a few hours, Jesus' lifeless body will be pierced with a spear. At the same moment, the thieves' legs are broken to hasten their deaths. Jesus will be buried in a borrowed tomb and his followers will quietly reassemble in an upper room in Jerusalem. These erstwhile disciples will be convinced they need to figure out how to go back to life as it was before Jesus called them to follow.

It looks a lot like the end of a tragic story. Appearances can be deceiving.

Questions to think about:
1. What does it feel like to have someone important remember you?
2. What did the criminal mean when he asked Jesus to "remember me when you come into your kingdom"?
3. Do you think it's right to see the cross as Jesus' throne? Why / why not?
4. Have you ever been so low that all you had left was faith? What would that be like?

Luke 24:1-12

The resurrection narrative starts with this glorious word, "But." In Greek it's a tiny, indeterminate connecting word, not the conjunction that implies a clear contrast. That's correct, of course; the crucifixion and resurrection (as well as Jesus' entire ministry) are a continuous outworking of God's necessity and plan. It's not like Satan won the crucifixion, but now Jesus is going to win the resurrection, even though it sometimes gets preached like that.

And yet, in the experience of the disciples, and probably in our experience as well, there is a marked contrast. "But" is not too strong a way to transition into this resurrection story. J.R.R. Tolkien talks about the gospel story being the most supreme and most true example of a fantasy story. In his remarkable essay "On Fairy Stories" he says that every good fantasy story includes the "dyscatastrophe" of tragedy. Then it also includes a turn, a "eucatastrophe" of joy. I want to quote Tolkien here at some length:

> The consolation of fairy-stories, of the joy of the happy ending: or more correctly of the good catastrophe, the sudden joyous 'turn' (for there is no true end to any fairy-tale): this joy, which is one of the things which fairy-stories can produce supremely well, is not essentially 'escapist' nor 'fugitive.' In its fairy-tale–or other-world–setting, it is a sudden and miraculous grace: never to be counted on to recur. It does not deny the idea of dyscatastrophe, of sorrow and failure: the possibility of these is necessary to the joy of deliverance; it denies (in the face of much evidence, if you will) universal final defeat and in so far is *evangelium*, giving a fleeting glimpse of Joy, Joy beyond the walls of the world, poignant as grief.[1]

We must enter into the gospel story enough to experience the depth of grief, of "dyscatastrophe" that the disciples, huddled in fear in an upper room, are experiencing. If we do not, then we will never receive the fullness of the resurrection. If we cannot bring our own grief and tragedy into the story, the resurrection will remain outside of us.

---

[1] JRR Tolkien, "On Fairy Stories"

This small conjunction, "But," holds for us the turning of the story. Dyscatastrophe becomes eucatastrophe; sorrow is turned shockingly to joy. The women come to the tomb and experience something quite different than they had expected. The angels announce to them, just as they announced to the shepherds at Jesus' birth, an amazing truth beyond the expected continuation of tragedy, oppression, and fear.

Our grief seems so permanent to us. Our fears and our frustrations dominate our days. If you have walked through grief, separation, and longing, you can feel the weight like gravestones on the hearts of the women as they walk to the tomb. Jesus is dead, and with him their hope. The announcement of the angels rings like breaking chains.

A word here about endurance. The greater the surprise in God's word to us, the clearer he will communicate. If God is asking you to do something surprising, he will make that direction clear. And like with Moses' objections or Gideon's fleece, he will be patient with your discernment. Jesus is so tenderly patient with those who need a moment to adjust to his resurrection. But once he has made that new direction clear, his voice will fade. He is still patient, but he will not continue to provide signs and speak in the silence of your heart to confront each doubt. Having revealed himself, he will ask you to trust him. This is why the remainder of the New Testament speaks so much and so eloquently about endurance. Now that we know the risen Christ, we endure the waiting for the fulfillment of his Kingdom.

As for the women at the tomb, the meantime is often fraught with confusion. Though they go and announce their disorienting experience, the rest of the disciples can't receive it. They reject the idea as an idle tale. Don't let the confusion of others dissuade you from all Jesus has spoken to you. In his own good time, Jesus will reveal himself to the others.

<u>Questions to think about:</u>
1. What would you say has been the most joyful moment of your life thus far? Why?
2. What do you think is the relationship between tragedy and joy?
3. Do you agree that if we do not enter into grief, we will never receive the fullness of the resurrection?
4. Has God ever asked you to do something surprising? Explain.

Luke 24:12-35

This narrative is one of the greatest stories in scripture. It overflows with heartbreak, humor, suspense, depth of character, and surprise. It is a masterful piece of flash non-fiction. Just a few examples of the amazing turns of phrase and poignant moments in this tiny episode:

"While they were talking and discussing together, Jesus himself drew near and went with them. But their eyes were kept from recognizing him." These two disciples (Cleopas and another unnamed disciple, quite possibly his wife) are talking things through. Processing their grief. Scrambling for purchase in the destabilizing events that surround them. Jesus comes near in their processing and walks with them, unrecognized. How often has Jesus walked with us and we have not recognized him?

"What things?" This is perhaps the funniest moment in the whole story. In Greek it's even more brief, just a single word: *Poia*? What things? They stagger under the things that have happened in Jerusalem concerning Jesus of Nazareth. What things? Think of all that is summed up in that phrase for them, going back to Jesus raising Lazarus from the dead and being honored with a banquet in his home; Jesus' triumphal entry on Palm Sunday; his teaching in the temple, his overthrowing of the money changers' tables; his furtive movements in and out of the city outwitting the Jewish authorities; the last supper in the upper room; the treason of Judas and Jesus' betrayal in the Garden of Gethsemane; the sham of a trial, shuffling back and forth from Annas to Caiaphas to Pilate to Herod and again to Pilate; the unthinkable flogging of the Son of God; the crown of thorns; the Via Dolorosa; the cross; Nicodemus and Joseph of Arimathea and others taking Jesus' lifeless body down and depositing it hastily in a new stone tomb; the disciples' huddling behind locked doors for fear. All this is summed up in their conversation. It is too much to process. But Jesus (who has been the heart of every event, every twist) asks, "What things?" as though he was a rube newly arrived from some backwater corner of the countryside. Can we see the humor that is an essential part of the joy that bubbles over?

"O foolish ones, and slow of heart to believe all that the prophets have spoken!" Jesus chastises these two for their unbelief, but then he goes on to instruct them. If there was ever a Bible study I wish I could be a part of, this is it. Jesus walks them through the Old Testament. He shows how all that has happened is not a discontinuation, not a disappointment, but is in fact the fulfillment of God's plan. How often I am slow of heart to believe all that God has promised! I get comfortable living in disappointment. I am too willing to be Eeyore in my thinking: This is all I can expect. I guess it will have to do. Instead, Jesus reminds them that God has a greater future planned. The trauma they've endured is part of the outworking of God's plan.

"And their eyes were opened, and they recognized him." There comes a moment when we see God's work for what it is. This is by grace, and nearly always surprises us. This moment, this new perspective, redefines the past. We see our own history clearly for the first time, redefining the events of our past. This moment reshapes the future in a flash, transforming it from more of the eternal same into a bright pathway of possibility. It is the splash of cold water on the face that wakes the sleeper. If we are too bound to our present perceptions, this will be an uncomfortable realization. If, however, we have learned to live with a God who is willing and eager to surprise his people with hope, we can ride this roller coaster with joy. Are you willing to let God surprise you?

"The Lord has risen indeed, and has appeared to Simon!" Apparently Jesus, after disappearing from the table at Emmaus, flashes to Jerusalem and has a conversation with Simon Peter. Peter then has time to inform the eleven and the others while Cleopas and his compatriot run the seven miles back to Jerusalem. This is news, not just information. (The distinction is ever so important.) Jesus spreads the fact of his resurrection around to various voices that then reinforce each other. Who is in your life with whom you can share resurrection stories? Who shares your hope? Who walks deeper into God's word, into possibility, into hope, with you?

Questions to think about:
1. What is one historical conversation you wish you could have witnessed?
2. Do you think God has a sense of humor? Explain.
3. What is it like to be surprised by God?
4. How does this story fly in the face of the skeptics' theory that Jesus never really died, but was simply revived in the cool air of the tomb?

Luke 24:36-53

Jesus gets the last word. He appears to his disciples yet again. His word is "Peace." The most common words God speaks in scripture are "don't be afraid" and "peace." The presence of God is a rock, an anchor, in the face of our fluttering daily anxieties. He is solid truth over against our vacillations. The resurrected Jesus, victorious over the grave and every other fear we face, speaks peace.

Imagine them in that room, groping with a new, expanded reality. Jesus reassures them in the face of what they thought was certain. His words are absolute treasures. "Why are you troubled? Why do you doubt?" Well, Jesus, you were dead just a bit ago. We're having trouble catching up. Just to make things harder to grasp, Jesus adds, "touch me and see my hands and feet, that it is I myself." At one level Jesus is dealing with their doubts. Yes, it's me. You can believe your eyes. This is not wishful thinking. The grander vision you've experienced is real.

At another level Jesus is speaking theologically, speaking about the truth of God. He says, "it is I myself" and in the Greek it is *ego eimi*. This just happens to be (as we have noted before) the exact words God uses to name himself to Moses. Jesus says "See my hands and feet, that I AM." The resurrected Jesus names himself as God, just in case we were starting to get our heads (and hearts) around the fact that he's alive in the first place. It's earthshaking.

I AM, who met Moses at the burning bush, who rescued the Israelites from Egypt, who placed David on the throne, who dropped fire on Mount Carmel at Elijah's word, who rescued the Jews from death through Esther's beautiful courage, I AM is risen from the grave. Death is no longer a period at the end of the sentence. At most it's a semi-colon. The story goes on for eternity.

Now, Jesus says, get to work. Repentance into the forgiveness of sins are to be proclaimed to all nations. What God promised when he called Abraham, that from this one new nation he would bring blessing to all the nations, is going to be fulfilled. Everyone is welcome. You've seen it; you've experienced it. Your testimony is important. As Jesus has welcomed you and spoken his love into your heart, go welcome and love the least, lost, broken ones. Proclaim life to those on the edges of death. Live the joy and gratitude that comes from being caught up in Jesus' resurrection. This is not the end of the story, not at all. It is only the beginning.

Questions to think about:
1. What is it like to experience the peace of God in times of high anxiety?
2. How is Christian hope, rooted in Jesus' resurrection, different from wishful thinking?
3. What does it mean that Jesus declares himself to be "I AM" in these verses?
4. How can Jesus' followers today be obedient to his command to proclaim repentance and forgiveness of sins to all nations? How can each of us do this?

Afterword

Jesus calls us to follow to the cross, to the empty tomb, and beyond. Luke is a stand-alone volume, but the story doesn't end there. Luke wrote a sequel we call "Acts." For us, too, the question is critically important: What will we do next? What will be our "acts" in response to Jesus?

For two thousand years, Christianity has endured the cycles of stale religion and Spirit-driven renewal. We live in a time of precipitous change. The Spirit is moving massively to bring people to new life in Jesus' name.

In the face of change, it can be comforting to find ourselves rooted in the biblical narrative. Be careful, though. It is easy to take our own excitement about Jesus and his new wineskins and let them grow cracked over time. Oswald Chambers has said that we receive revelation about God like hot lead, and then we pour it into molds where it cools. When it is cold and hard we throw it at our opponents.

If you have met Jesus, especially if you have met him in a new, life-giving way, hang on. Don't let that relationship become stale. Stay in his word. Don't confuse the wine of Jesus with the wineskins of your current practice. Don't try to follow him alone. Surround yourself with a community of people who will follow Jesus into the world with you. Live out the new wine of Jesus' love with them.

Peace.

New Wineskins

CPSIA information can be obtained
at www.ICGtesting.com
Printed in the USA
BVHW040727131221
623907BV00016B/732